CLUES
TJ605 Z55
CUM 00 0087368 Q
P9-DFC-997

Along the Banks of the Greenbrier

After an early winter snowfall a Heisler, crowned with a huge balloon stack in the manner of a century ago, is seen hightailing along the Chesapeake & Ohio at Beard, West Virginia. The old engine, en route to the Cass Scenic Railway, hugged the edge of the Greenbrier River for much of her trip. This move, which would have been rare even when steam ruled the rails, was made during the Christmas season of 1966.

Ron Ziel

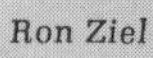

TJ
605
Z55
69-603
Ziel
Steam in the sixties
JUL 2000
JUN 2004
JUL X X 2015
WITHDRAWN

Michael A. Eagleson

STEAM IN THE SIXTIES

STEAM

Canadian National 4-8-4 No. 6218 in Maine.

Donald S. Robinson

IN THE SIXTIES

by Ron Ziel and George H. Foster

CUMBERLAND COUNTY COLLEGE
LIBRARY P.O. BOX 517 VINELAND N.J.

Meredith Press New York

TJ
605
Z55

69-603

Copyright © 1967 by Ron Ziel and George H. Foster
All rights reserved. No part of this book in excess of five hundred words may be reproduced in any form without permission in writing from the publisher.

First edition

Library of Congress Catalog Card Number: 67-24432
Manufactured in the United States of America for Meredith Press

Contents

U.S. Army 2-8-0 at Fort Eustis, Virginia.

Ron Ziel

It was with deep regret that rail historians, men of letters, and connoisseurs of the good life learned of the death of Lucius Beebe on February 4, 1966. During his sixty-three years Mr. Beebe became a symbol of the excellence which disappeared from the American scene during his lifetime. The coauthor of many of his railroad books, Charles Clegg, graciously sent the photo of Mr. Beebe taken at the Beebe, Arkansas, railroad station while they were gathering material for a book. Mr. Clegg found the unpublished manuscript, *opposite,* among Mr. Beebe's personal papers shortly after his death. It gives a good insight into the nature of the unique man and his high standards. The loss is great, and it is to the memory of Lucius Beebe that this volume is dedicated.

I have not cared greatly for or been impressed too urgently by people or what they do or want or think. I haven't known many but those I have have derived from, I think, the better vintages of professional competence. This is what has most impressed me and may well be a shallow thing, but I have admired most of all, competence, the quality of being strictly professional. This must be understood to extend to every aspect of living within the individual purview so that the business of having lived has been done, in all directions, with competence, its obligations discharged without blemish, its satisfactions achieved in the knowledge of their excellence.

Lucius Beebe

Ron Ziel

ACKNOWLEDGMENTS

We wish to thank Michael A. Eagleson; Wilbur T. Golson; Karl R. Koenig; Donald S. Robinson; Charles M. Clegg; John Gretton; Brad S. Miller; Richard Glueck; F. G. Zahn; Daniel A. Foley; Herschel Pike; Victor Hand; Vincent Alvino; W. Graham Claytor, Vice President-Law of the Southern Railway; Ernest Bourjaily and José Dolores Colunga, who greatly assisted the authors in Mexico; the management of the National Railways of Mexico; Ed Lewis of the Arcade & Attica; William Whitehead; Robert L. Havens; Edith M. Ziel; Dorothy H. Foster; Helen C. Foster; the shop crew of the Mid-Continent Railway Museum, for working until 5 A.M. to get their splendid 4-6-0 No. 1 operating for the authors' camera; Jerrie Schmitt and the many people among the railroad men, railfan fraternity and interested friends and acquaintances who gave of their time and talent to advise, assist and console the authors during the usual myriad frustrations which arise out of completing a book such as this.

Mexican Railfan

José Dolores Colunga, the authors' good friend and personal guide, who, as an employee of the National Railways of Mexico and with his bilingual abilities, wás of assistance beyond all description.

Gene Collora

On the Ready Track

Canadian National No. 6218 shares the engine terminal at New London, Connecticut, with a brace of diesels, *above*. It is 4 A.M. on a spring morning in 1967, and the big Northern is resting prior to hauling a fantrip up the Connecticut valley.

NO TRESPASSING

The End of Big Steam

By the time 1960 arrived, all of the main-line steam operations were past in America, and thousands of locomotives stood rusting on various storage tracks. Although some would be preserved by museums, the vast majority were doomed to the scrapper's torch. A precious few, such as the Pennsylvania Railroad's last M-1 4-8-2, shown here awaiting disposition at Northumberland, Pennsylvania, could perhaps look forward to operating once more at some distant date.

Michael A. Eagleson

Introduction

With the dawn of manned space flight in the 1960's, the steam locomotive has become the dinosaur of the Space Age. Scarcely thirty years before, the diesel-electric power which replaced steam was a technological curiosity; only ten years before, 60 percent of all railroad movements were still steam-powered. By 1958 only

Michael A. Eagleson

Nickel Plate; Duluth, Missabe & Iron Range; Illinois Central; Grand Trunk Western; Union Pacific; and the last holdout, Norfolk & Western, still dispatched tonnage in quantity behind steam locomotives. A few roads, notably the Chicago, Burlington & Quincy and the Reading, possessed serviceable steam power to haul fan trips after 1959, the year that Union Pacific's great Challengers and Big Boys last saw service. Early in 1960 the Norfolk & Western completed a three-year crash program of dieselizing the entire system. During this same period Canadian Pacific received a large fleet of new diesels, and steam was banished from active service north of Latin America. In Mexico large steam movements were still evident, but even these would soon be gone.

For many a rail enthusiast and most railroad men, steam in the 1960's meant little tank switchers and narrow-gauge Mikados dressed up in green paint and phony balloon stacks, running to nowhere and back, carrying tourists who delighted at staged "Indian raids." This nonsense meant money for promoters, amusement for those of dubious taste, and a completely warped sense of history for youngsters exposed to it. It also thoroughly disgusted rail historians and many other people who recalled the huge black locomotives which had been objects of awe in their youthful years.

Fortunately there was much more to steam in the sixties. Although by 1965 the frustrated steam buff was able to count the number of "active" (one to ten days annually) main-line steamers on the fingers of his two hands, a diligent search could still ferret out scores of steam locomotives in short-line, industrial, and switching service, as well as many preserved and operated by serious railroad men and fans. In a sense, this volume tells the story of a few of the most active steam photographers who have traveled so far to record on celluloid a contraption which was the most common of public conveyances a very few years previously. Indeed, of the seven photographers whose work forms 98 percent of this book, three have traveled well over 100,000 miles each in search of the debris of dieselization. The other four have run up impressive mileages as well.

William Jackson, Colonel Savage and Matthew Brady, with their wet-plate techniques of the late

---

The Last Moments

The earliest months of the 1960's witnessed the final demise of "big steam." On April 4, 1960, Norfolk & Western dropped the fires in the last of its great Y-6 2-8-8-2's and S-1 0-8-0's, *above*, at Roanoke, Virginia. It was all over at last to the disbelief of even the foremost diesel partisans.

Three photos, George H. Foster

The Quick and the Dead

Years after they last operated, some locomotives rested on rip tracks and backwoods spurs in the most disgraceful condition imaginable. A view beyond the rusty firebox doors of a long-forgotten Illinois Central switch engine, *above*, reveals daylight showing through the firebox, long after the 0-6-0's boiler has been disassembled. Steam still filled some cylinders on such fan operations as the Wanamaker, Kempton & Southern, *right*, and there still could be found that rarity in steam, the locomotive in regular freight service. On a cold morning in early spring, 2-8-2 No. 31 of the Rockton & Rion, *upper right*, backs down to switching chores at a stone crusher in Rion, South Carolina.

1800's, and Lucius Beebe, O. Winston Link, Jim Shaugnessey, and a host of others in the past generation contributed to the archives of the steam age; but the men whose work is here recorded have preserved what can no longer even be called the twilight of steam. For them, the afterglow has vanished with the last plume of coal smoke on the western horizon. Eternal night has descended upon abandoned roundhouses whose very rafters contain the saga of steam in the soot left by hundreds of thousands of locomotives.

Steam in the sixties, then, was a time of anguish and frustration, as those who had reveled in the age of steam reconciled themselves to the fact of total dieselization. It was a time of expectation when, for a brief moment, the faithful could yet head north or south to recapture the operation of main-line steam on film and recording tape. There were times of great relief: Reading deferred retirement of its last steamers for another season; rumors of the end in Mexico were discounted by returning railfan *turistas*. There was even time for jubilation: the Buffalo Creek & Gauley would reopen in steam after its abandonment, and fans, pondering the huge locomotives preserved by the Union Pacific, happily

480

speculated on how that road would celebrate the Golden Spike Centennial on May 10, 1969.

By the mid-sixties every steam movement in the United States was attended by swarms of curious viewers and escorted by legions of automobiles, while airborne photographers in rented Cessnas circled overhead. So steam-starved had the railfans become that some literally traveled cross-country to ride behind a locomotive they had not previously seen. Inevitably the public press caught on, and the long wake over the steam era was well reported.

As the number of revenue steam locomotives neared extinction the combination of awareness of this fact and interest by news media spurred various "preservation" groups and individuals to action. Social pressure and the promise of sellout trips encouraged enlightened railroad managements to take the business risks necessary to operate steam excursions. Rail historians, as groups and individuals, bought or accepted donated steam engines, with plans for eventual operation. Seizing a lucrative chance, opportunistic promoters purchased modern locomotives and went through elaborate processes to give them an "antique" look—to the delight of the barbaric tastes of the uninitiated public, who fancied that an engine built in 1943 was the ideal means of transport to an "Indian attack" staged by local misfits just around the next curve.

Whatever their reason for operating, steam locomotives were scattered throughout the land and were still prolific beyond the North American continent as the 1960's neared an end. Here is recorded their passing, by spectators who have turned an interesting avocation into an historical chronicling. Those who prematurely wrote steam's epitaph in the late 1950's had not reckoned with the elaborate events that were to mark the course of steam in the sixties.

Tenacious Narrow Gauge
The narrow-gauge division of the Denver & Rio Grande Western Railway, a three-hundred-mile stretch which runs from Colorado into New Mexico, was the last stronghold of steam in America. By 1967, however, the railroad had managed to transfer most of the freight to trucks, a prelude to the demise of this delightfully anachronistic operation. Nowhere else in the "growling" sixties could this scene of four locomotives under steam in the snows of winter be seen. This was Chama, New Mexico, in January, 1963.

Ron Ziel

Michael A. Eagleson

Ron Ziel

Beyond American Borders

By coincidence, the Canadian Pacific retired the last of its steam power within weeks of dieselization on the Norfolk & Western. Sister system Canadian National dropped its fires at the same time, and from the harbor at Halifax to Kicking Horse Pass, the steam locomotives were gathered in and dispatched to the scrappers. A variety of locomotives were still stored in serviceable condition, however, and could be called out for fan trips. Pacific No. 5107, *above*, pulled an excursion across the Richelieu River at St. Hilaire, Quebec, on the Canadian National in the autumn of 1962. The situation in Mexico was more favorable. There big steam movements were still to be seen into the late sixties, but in ever-dwindling numbers, until this last citadel of steam power in North America yielded to the diesel onslaught. One of the National Railways of Mexico's famous 4-8-4 Niagaras, *left*, the last active class of standard-gauge steam on the continent, heads north from Mexico City with a merchandise extra.

Two photos, Ron Ziel

Donald S. Robinson

Last of Their Breeds

With the dieselization of the Mississippian and Rockton & Rion Railways in mid-1967, only the Reader Railroad, in deepest Arkansas, carried on an appreciable steam operation in the Deep South. Its two spotless Prairie locomotives, *lower left*, are shown peddling out to the Reader main on a spring morning. In Wanamie, near Scranton, Pennsylvania, several narrow-gauge 0-4-0T's, including No. 8, *left*, still moved mining cars in the operational manner of a century before. The cars were loosely chained together and the wooden buffers at the ends of each car were rapped at every move. The Wanamie operation was still going strong when this photo was taken, on January 23, 1967, the last of the Lokie mining operations which were once prevalent all through the coal regions of Pennsylvania. One of the oldest and best-known tourist railroads is the Edaville, in South Carver, Massachusetts. Employing the remaining equipment of the little two-foot gauge railroads which operated in Maine until the World War II era, the Edaville is one of millionaire-railfan F. Nelson Blount's enterprises. Unfortunately, the original appearance, *above*, of four little engines has been destroyed in an attempt to give them a nineteenth-century look as they run over five miles of track in the Cape Cod cranberry bogs.

Two photos, George H. Foster

Ron Ziel

The Loons Take Over

Some railfans jokingly call themselves loons, and the uninitiated will undoubtedly concur. A loon may peer from a baggage-car door during a photo run-past, pursue a steam train in his automobile, or otherwise behave in a manner common to all in this esoteric fraternity. The term is good-naturedly self-inflicted, and in the postmortem of the steam age these loons are everywhere in the land, pursuing their iron quarry and frequently being pursued in turn by the highway patrol. Here they are in action on the Southern Railway, *above,* in Virginia; the Jersey Central, *above right,* in Pennsylvania; the Union Pacific, *right,* in Wyoming.

Main Line

Once the "Big Show" was over, main-line activity was restricted to occasional fan trips. A few stubborn branch lines owned by class-one roads, in contrast to small, independent short lines, survived under steam. By 1962 the last of these branches was dieselized, and a half-dozen 4-8-4's and 4-6-2's, plus one 2-8-2, inherited the title "Main-line Power" from over 200,000 predecessors over the past 135 years.

Fortunately the situation improved with the coming of the paradoxical "Main-line Branchline" locomotives of the mid-sixties. It became the vogue for owners of small Consolidations and Canadian Pacific ten-wheelers to trot out these short-haul machines and run them around one-hundred-car freights, commuter trains, and Budd Rail Diesel Cars. This was a novel approach indeed and required a degree of courage and foresight not normally found in present-day railroad management. Passengers found it wise to look askance at the announced schedule, but it was a delightful—and usually successful—experiment which held great promise.

Class-One Steam Exits

When the Grand Trunk Western, a subsidiary of the Canadian National, dieselized the last regularly scheduled steam passenger train in America in 1960, its freight service suffered the same fate. That left only one of the most romantic and inaccessible branch lines in steam. The Colorado & Southern saw fit to keep the desolate and historical Climax spur to Leadville, Colorado, steam-powered until October 11, 1962, which marked the cessation of class-one steam in regular service in the United States. Extra 641 East is shown leaving the eleven-thousand-foot-altitude yard at Leadville behind the venerable Colorado & Southern 2-8-0, No. 641. Twelve days later the diesel replacement shoved the Consolidation onto a display pedestal in Leadville.

Donald S. Robinson

2124
READING

Two photos, Ron Ziel

Northerns East and West

Probably the most famous steam engines in the country during the early 1960's were three Reading T-1 class 4-8-4 Northerns, Nos. 2100, 2102, and 2124. Between 1959 and 1964 these locomotives, operating singly or double-heading, carried over fifty thousand passengers on fifty-one "Iron Horse Rambles" through New Jersey and Pennsylvania. One even pulled trips on the Baltimore & Ohio. Since 1964 the 2100 and 2102 have been stored by the Reading, while 2124 has gone to permanent preservation at Steamtown, Vermont. The newest steam locomotive (American Locomotive Company, 1944) to operate on the Union Pacific was No. 844, the last of U.P.'s great class of 4-8-4's. She is shown here on the memorable journey of September 1, 1963, when she pulled a National Railway Historical Society Convention Special over Sherman Hill, between Cheyenne and Laramie, Wyoming.

Vincent Alvino

Two photos, Ron Ziel

Two Great Ladies

From Chicago to Denver there was one great Granger locomotive which wrote the final chapter to steam in the Midwest. Built by the Chicago, Burlington & Quincy's own West Burlington shops in 1940, 0-5B No. 5632 was the last survivor of her class to see service. She is shown, *above and right,* wheeling on Santa Fe trackage between Denver and Colorado Springs in 1963. One of the last engines of the classic Georgian design which was so prevalent on the rosters of Dixie in steam's Golden Age, Savannah & Atlanta 4-6-2 No. 750, *upper left,* is now owned by the Atlanta Chapter of the N.R.H.S. Apparently thriving on the soot and cinders of sixty miles per hour, the riders on the tender are reliving the great days now past, as the fifty-six-year-old Pacific pulls the 1966 Independence Day Georgia Peach Special over the Southern main near Flovilla, Georgia.

Michael A. Eagleson

Three photos, Ron Ziel

"When You're out of Schlitz—You're out of Steam!" After the retirement of Chicago, Burlington & Quincy No. 5632 and her subsequent sale to a railfan for eleven thousand dollars, the last steam engine owned by a class-one railway east of the Rocky Mountains, the "Q's" 2-8-2 No. 4960, made her final run on the Burlington on July 17, 1966. Although retiring president H. C. Murphy had approved the rebuilding of both engines, his successor, L. W. Menk (*Modern Railroads'* "Man of the Year") vetoed the project. The 4960 was donated to the Circus World Museum at Baraboo, Wisconsin. This organization, in conjunction with the Schlitz Brewing Company, operated an annual circus train between Baraboo and Milwaukee, powered by the 4960. They announced plans to keep the Mikado running. There was much grumbling among fans who wondered why one of the nation's most prosperous railroads could not afford to maintain one live steamer, while a brewery could. One group even distributed "Menk Is a Fink" buttons. A. M. Rung, C.B.&Q. Director of Public Relations, assured the authors of this volume that the decision to kill steam was not made lightly, and that the cost of maintaining the engines for the five years ending January 1, 1966, had been $95,817 above trip revenues, which included the $42,774 collected for the Steam Preservation Fund by the simple expedient of charging one dollar more per ticket on steam trips. Both sides had valid arguments, and fortunately the new owners of both locomotives hoped to operate them. The center of the controversy, No. 4960, is shown here in her last month of Burlington operation. On June 12, 1966, she met a diesel freight at Zearing, Illinois, *above,* while powering an Illini Railroad Club Special. On July 1 the Mike passed Lodi, Wisconsin, *left,* and continued along the Chicago & North Western trackage, *below,* near Helenville, en route to Milwaukee with the fascinating Schlitz Circus Train.

1910

Steam on the New Haven

When the famous Civil War engine *General* steamed over the Hell Gate Bridge and down the New York Connecting Railroad, *above,* to the Long Island Rail Road on May 30, 1964, it marked the first steam movement on the New Haven in eleven years and on the Long Island in nine years. The 108-year-old 4-4-0 was en route to a display pedestal at the New York World's Fair. Little 2-8-0 No. 97 (ex-Birmingham & Southeastern No. 200) also made its way to New Haven rails. She is shown pulling a fan trip, *left,* through the tunnel at Terryville, Connecticut, on October 30, 1966, during a hectic and frustrating main-line run. In more appropriate surroundings the 97 operated on the Vermont Railway, *below,* near North Bennington the previous year.

Donald S. Robinson

Two photos, Michael A. Eagleson

The Green Mountain Railway

The biggest steam news of the 1960's was the operation of New England millionaire-railfan F. Nelson Blount. In the late 1950's Blount began acquiring locomotives until he had amassed a collection of eighty-five by 1967—with more being added. The engines were scattered all over the world, but a home for at least part of the collection was being constructed at Bellows Falls, Vermont, on the west bank of the Connecticut River. Here Steamtown, U.S.A., the multimillion-dollar museum, was taking shape. This is a nonprofit foundation and Blount is donating the engines, whose acquisition and movement have cost him over two million dollars. When the state of Vermont purchased the defunct Rutland Railway, it turned operating rights of the fifty-two mile Rutland–Bellows Falls branch over to Blount's Green Mountain Railway. He operates both diesel freights and steam passenger excursions over the system, which is rapidly becoming one of New England's most important tourist attractions. A doubleheader with 2-8-0 No. 15 and 4-6-2 No. 127 is shown, *below*, and 2-6-0 No. 89, *right*, in Rutland.

Michael A. Eagleson, lighting by Victor Hand

Ron Ziel

89
89

Steam's Promising Future

Because of prior planning which included the acquisition of duplicate locomotives of certain classes and the stockpiling of spare parts, Steamtown may prove to be the biggest operator of main-line steam power in North America, virtually becoming a monopoly just as General Motors has become with the manufacture of diesels. A major step in that direction was achieved on October 16, 1966, when No. 127, an ex-C.P.R. light Pacific, was sent to Jersey City to pull two trips for the High Iron Company on the Central Railroad of New Jersey. This trip, under the direction of Ross Rowland and Bill Whitehead, turned out to be one of the best fan trips that the authors have ever had the pleasure of riding. The plucky 4-6-2, *left*, moved a baggage car, eleven coaches, and Sag Harbor & Scuttle Hole Rail Road private car No. 97 (the *Havpalm*) to Jim Thorpe, Pennsylvania, and back with ease. With the success of this run and an identical one the following week, other eastern railroads expressed an interest in such trips, and Blount sent a heavy 4-6-2 into the shops. Eventually to join the growing roster of operating big steam was Nickel Plate 2-8-4 Berkshire No. 759, which, in addition to hauling passenger trains, may see freight service on the Green Mountain Railway. The best was clearly to come. One of the Steamtown engines was scheduled to go on a national tour with a visiting British locomotive in 1968. Mogul No. 89, *below*, interrupted a college fraternity party as she crossed a high bridge on the Vermont Railway —formerly the Rutland Line from Burlington to Bennington.

Two photos, Ron Ziel

Michael A. Eagleson

Ron Ziel

A Resurrection of the Finest in Steam

When the Southern Railway ordered its fleet of great PS-4 Pacifics in 1924, they were painted apple-green with gold trim, and they had gray smokeboxes with burnished rods and red tank tops and cab roofs. This fleet of locomotives gained fame as being one of the most beautiful in the world. Regrettably all of the PS-4's except the 1401, now displayed at the Smithsonian Institution in Washington, D.C., have been scrapped, but thanks to the energetic efforts of W. Graham Claytor, Legal Vice President of the Southern, and of D. W. Brosnan, President, and the Tennessee Valley Railroad Museum, a grand facsimile is now operating. For many years an ex-Southern 2-8-2, *above*, had been running out of Stearns, Kentucky, as No. 12 of the coal-hauling Kentucky & Tennessee Railway. When the K. & T. dieselized in 1963 No. 12 was acquired by the Tennessee Valley Museum and given its original Southern number, 4501. Graham Claytor prevailed upon the Southern to operate the 1911 Mikado, and she received a complete overhaul, including a paint scheme identical to the legendary PS-4's. Since then the 4501 has come a long way from the soot and oblivion of Kentucky coal freights. Now the prima donna of the Southern, the 4501 is expected to have years of fan-trip service ahead of her.

"The Steam Locomotive Is Here to Stay."

W. Graham Claytor, Jr., Vice-President—Law, Southern Railway. From the banquet speech of the N.R.H.S. Convention, Richmond, Virginia, September 3, 1966

George H. Foster

In Southern Tradition

Mikado No. 4501 is shown on the Manassas branch, *above,* and climbing the grade near Green Bay, Virginia, *right.* The "bucket brigade" method of coaling the green and gold Mike was used at Burkeville, *below,* on the trip from Richmond to Keysville, Virginia, during the 1966 N.R.H.S. National Convention.

Two photos, Ron Ziel

Narrow-Gauge Through the Rockies

Reams of copy have been written in recent years concerning the Denver & Rio Grande Western narrow-gauge operations in Colorado and New Mexico. Suffice it to say that this was the most unique railroad in the United States during the 1960's. Here were almost three hundred miles of three-foot-gauge track, comprising the only common-carrier narrow-gauge operation in the continental United States. Except for the Durango Switcher, the line was 100 percent steam-powered by a fleet of Baldwin outside-frame Mikados. The rest of its equipment was just as fascinating. Solid seventy-car trains of pre-1900 freight cars were dispatched over 10,015-foot Cumbres Pass right through the mid-sixties. The branch from Durango to Silverton, Colorado, covered elsewhere in this volume, had become one of the most successful passenger runs in the nation. By 1967, alas, Rio Grande trucks were able to handle most of the freight, and although extensive track improvements were underway, the narrow gauge, with the sole exception of the Silverton branch, had come upon precarious days indeed.

Two photos, Ron Ziel

Winter Freights

It was impossible to see scenes such as these winter freight operations anywhere in the Western Hemisphere during the 1960's except on the Denver & Rio Grande Western. On a January evening in 1963, with the temperature at 22 degrees below zero, 2-8-2's Nos. 492 and 484, *left,* kept vigil through the cold night at the engine terminal yard of Chama, New Mexico. Double-heading toward Cumbres Pass from Gato, *above,* No. 492, with helper 491, charges the steep grade with fifty-seven cars of mixed freight and gas pipe in tow.

Ron Ziel

Robert E. Ziel

System-wide Fan Trips

During the sunset years of the narrow gauge, many long trips, taking three to five days, were operated over the line from Alamosa to Durango, along the Farmington and Silverton branches. Business organizations from Alamosa, railfan groups from Denver, and others ran these trips as annual events. The Illini Railroad Club, an Illinois-based group, sponsored an annual Journey to Yesterday to the narrow gauge, which took over a week and was one of the best trips offered anywhere. The run from Alamosa to Durango took one day, with a day each on the Silverton and Farmington branches, returning on the fourth day. On the 1966 Illini trip the extra rounded Cumbres Loop, *left*. Passengers in the open excursion car, *above*, enjoyed a good view of engine 483 as it took them around the reverse curves down the east slope of Cumbres.

487

Three photos, Ron Ziel

The Broad-reaching Narrow Gauge

Engine No. 487, a snowplow mounted on her pilot, passes a water tower, *left,* on the Farmington branch in New Mexico in 1962. A passenger extra, *above,* is rounding a curve at milepost 313.5 in June, 1966, behind No. 483. Four years earlier the Illini Special, *below,* crosses a truss bridge en route to Durango.

Snow Train over Cumbres

One of the most interesting movements in American railroading was that of the snow-removal trains which the Denver & Rio Grande Western dispatched from Alamosa to Chama until the demise of winter operations. Few outsiders ever saw this operation, yet it was the epitome of steam railroading. Locomotives, cold, snow, spreaders, steam-powered snow flangers, and a steam-powered freight just one hour behind made this a railroader's dream! A view from the fireman's seat, *left,* shows the spreader in action. The two engines on the ascent to Cumbres, *right,* are seen from the cupola of the rear hack. The snow train rounding Cumbres Loop, *below,* makes a lonely run in a cold, hostile land.

Three photos, Ron Ziel

Rebirth of an Institution

After the Civil War, particularly in the former Confederacy, hundreds of small railroads were constructed to connect industrial areas, towns, or mines with the main lines or branches of class-one carriers. These short lines varied in length from one or two miles to over one hundred miles and usually dispatched but one train daily down the light rails whose rights-of-way held such fascination for rail enthusiasts. Before the rise of individual mobility brought to the American scene by the automobile, most of these lines offered passenger service in the form of a combine and, perhaps, a coach coupled at the end of the freight cars. The mixed-consist trains were slow, schedules were often irregular, and the passengers had to wait while the locomotive switched all of the sidings along the route. With the passing of the leisurely way of life, the short-line mixed train went into slow decline, until, by 1962, only one remained in the United States—and it was usually diesel-powered. It is a happy circumstance, indeed, that has brought about a revival of that hallowed institution, the mixed train, in the mid-1960's. Paced by the progressive Reader Railroad in Arkansas, which added passenger equipment to its freight trains on a regular schedule in December, 1962, several other common-carrier steam freight roads are venturing into this profitable new field.

Even while the last steam-powered mixed trains were phased out of class-one service in North America, these new operations carried on the tradition of trains so unique, so vital to their immediate areas, and so reflective of the folk who used their service, that they inspired the late Lucius Beebe to write what was perhaps his greatest work.* The mixed train, in the sixties, was enjoying a renaissance of modest proportions as more railroads, both common-carrier and amusement type, contemplated the operation of similar equipment.

Mixed Train Daily, E. P. Dutton & Co., New York, 1947.

Great Lakes Mixed Trains

Away up in northern Wisconsin the Laona & Northern runs steam-powered mixed trains during the summer months. Basically a fine operation, the L. & N. unfortunately has lettered an immature "4-Spot" on the cab of 2-6-2 No. 4, *above.* The Cadillac & Lake City, operating between the towns of its corporate title in central Michigan, *right,* deals mostly in timber products and passengers, like the Laona & Northern. Reminiscent of the winter snows she knew during nearly fifty years of service on the Canadian National, 4-6-0 No. 1533, *below,* runs through a Pennsylvania snowfall on February 13, 1967, pulling a boxcar and a coach for her new owner, the New Hope & Ivyland Railroad.

Three photos, Ron Ziel

Wilbur T. Golson

The Last of the Original Mixtos
Of the hundreds of mixed trains which graced the *Official Guide* over nearly a century, about half were operated by short lines. The rest were branches of class-one roads which, more frequently than not, were indistinguishable from the class-two and class-three roads in quaint operating procedures and informality. Coincidentally, and juxtaposed to the rise of the new generation of mixtos, the last steam-powered short line and the last steam class-one mixed trains were dieselized in 1964. Mogul No. 20, *above,* of East Texas' Moscow, Camden & San Augustine, and Mikado No. 14, *left,* are shown at Camden in the early sixties. Photographed but a few months before dieselization, on July 28, 1964, National Railways of Mexico's last standard-gauge steam mixto is making its way down the flimsy iron of the Jaral del Progreso branch, *right,* behind a light 2-8-2, No. 2103. In later years the Mexican English-language timetables indicated if the trains were steam-powered. Trains 228 and 227, the Irapuato-Salamanca-Escobedo local mixto, shown here, were also the last standard-gauge trains so listed.

Three photos, Ron Ziel

George H. Foster

Wilbur T. Golson

Mixed Train par Excellence

The aristocrat and, although only five years old, the patriarch of latter-day mixed trains is the thrice-weekly run of the 23.5-mile Reader Railroad in Arkansas. Known for its spotless brace of 2-6-2's (page 20), the Reader acquired a 1942 War Department 2-8-0 from the nearby Warren & Saline River, *above,* in 1964. The engine was completely rebuilt in the Reader's primitive shop and emerged handsomer than anybody acquainted with the dismally utilitarian Army 2-8-0's would have believed possible. She now sports a classy pilot, acquired in Mexico from an ex-Florida East Coast 4-8-2, a Texas & Pacific headlight, a Kansas City Southern turbogenerator, and a Cotton Belt whistle. Reader Chief Mechanical Officer J. K. Byrne and his men completely rebuilt the G.I. Consolidation in two and a half months of sixteen-hour working days, seven days a week, just in time for her to star in the motion picture, *This Property Is Condemned.* Editor David P. Morgan of *Trains Magazine* stood by while his wife Margaret christened the 1702, *right,* with French champagne, and Reader's dynamic President T. W. M. Long ducked. On this memorable April 4, 1966, the 1702 obligingly showed off, *left,* for her admirers during the photo run-past which is a normal part of each southbound trip. The patrician appearance of the most deluxe of mixed accommodations is readily evident, *below,* as 1702 switches the passenger cars prior to assembling her train of tank cars at Waterloo, Arkansas.

Two photos, Ron Ziel

South of the Border

Steam in Central Mexico was still relatively common ten years after dieselization in English-speaking North America. In the early 1960's Hudsons, Pacifics, 2-6-6-2's, and a brace of ex-Norfolk Southern 2-8-4's were still to be seen. Some were used in passenger service. By 1964 only one standard-gauge steam train moved passengers, but all of the helpers and 60 percent of the freights operating north out of Mexico City were under steam. However, the last pairs of 4-8-2's and 4-8-0's and the last trio of 2-8-0's were on the verge of retirement by diesels. A year later the great fleet of 2-8-2's was silenced along with twelve of the handsome 4-8-4 Niagaras, outshopped in 1946. As late as March 23, 1966, a photographer could record a 4-8-4, *below*, emerging from *Túnel Barrientos* north of the *Valle de Mexico* terminal, oblivious to the technology which had retired hundreds of her sisters—leaving merely twenty of her class in the sixties. In happier days, *right*, just twenty-one months earlier, steam still helped steam tackle the grades northbound from Tula.

The narrow-gauge lines south and east of the capital were still largely traversed by outside-frame Consolidations, but three-foot-gauge diesels finished off the last 4-6-0's in 1964. In the spring of 1966 track crews began placing standard-gauge ties under the narrow-gauge rails. The end was indeed at hand.

Two photos, Ron Ziel

Three photos, Ron Ziel

Valle Norte

During the last five years of steam power on the standard-gauge Ferrocarriles Nacionales de Mexico—the National Railways of Mexico—movements were dispatched from the roundhouse at Valle de Mexico, the big yard in the northernmost suburbs of the capital city. There, in late summer of 1964, over one hundred steam locomotives of five different wheel arrangements and several subclasses were still in service. *Above,* one of the last three 2-8-0's, No. 1137, leaves the roundhouse to begin her daily chores in yard switching service. *Below,* 4-8-4 No. 3053, running northbound, light passes 2-8-2 No. 2141, assigned to the local Tula freight. After having been sideswiped, No. 3038, *right,* is being overhauled in the Valle roundhouse. Here a welder works on a connecting rod.

¡Adios, Locomotoras de Vapor!

To the *norteamericanos* who visited the shops at Valle the phrases *locomotora de vapor* and *casa de máquinas* (meaning steam locomotive and roundhouse) were all the knowledge of Spanish necessary to lead them to the last sanctuary of heavy steam power on the continent. Here, just a few months before their retirement, the last operating 4-8-2 Mountain types in North America, N.deM. Nos. 3306, *above,* and 3316, *below,* (joined by 2-8-2 No. 2134 in a confrontation with two diesels) fussed about the yard, impatiently awaiting assignments to northbound local freights. With the next diesel delivery putting 4-8-0 No. 3000 to the torch, the last twelve-wheeler, No. 3002, *right,* a Baldwin product of 1936, took on sand before being called to pull what was to be the longest freight the authors were to see in Mexico—forty-four cars.

Three photos, Ron Ziel

3002

RIA
ELUQUERIA
EL
ZODEORO

Hardworking Mikados

The majority of locomotives on the N.de M. roster were of United States manufacture. By the 1960's all of the European engines were gone, but much secondhand power was still in service, including Illinois Central ten-wheelers. The 4-8-2's were classic United States Railway Administration light Mountains which had been built for the Florida East Coast Railway. All of the 2200-series 2-8-2's, such as No. 2213, *left*, were purchased from the Nickel Plate Road at the close of World War II. Far from the level plains of Ohio, this N.K.P. Mikado works a long stone train up the grade toward the tunnel north of Mexico City, while one of N.de M.'s own Mikes, No. 2141, leaves Tula during one of the cloudbursts so common to Mexican summer afternoons.

Two photos, Ron Ziel

Ron Ziel

Friend and Compatriot

Mexico, as a nation, is very aware of the role which the railroads have played in its development. The popular rebellion of 1910 saw the protagonists of both sides utilizing the mobility of the rails, and the huge murals depicting the revolution in modern Mexico show steam locomotives in the midst of battle scenes. In a country where few people can afford automobiles and good roads are scarce, travel by rail is as common now as it was in the United States during the World War I era. Of course, the Mexican railways are one of the largest employers as well. Until the end of steam the railroad was the only source of clean water in many towns, either from the tanks, which were fed by deep wells, or from the locomotives themselves. A young girl, *left*, is assured of uncontaminated water, courtesy of a Niagara. In the narrow-gauge yard at San Lázaro, *above*, roundhouse workers, as they have for seventy years, provide the power for the turntable at the moment of dieselization.

George H. Foster

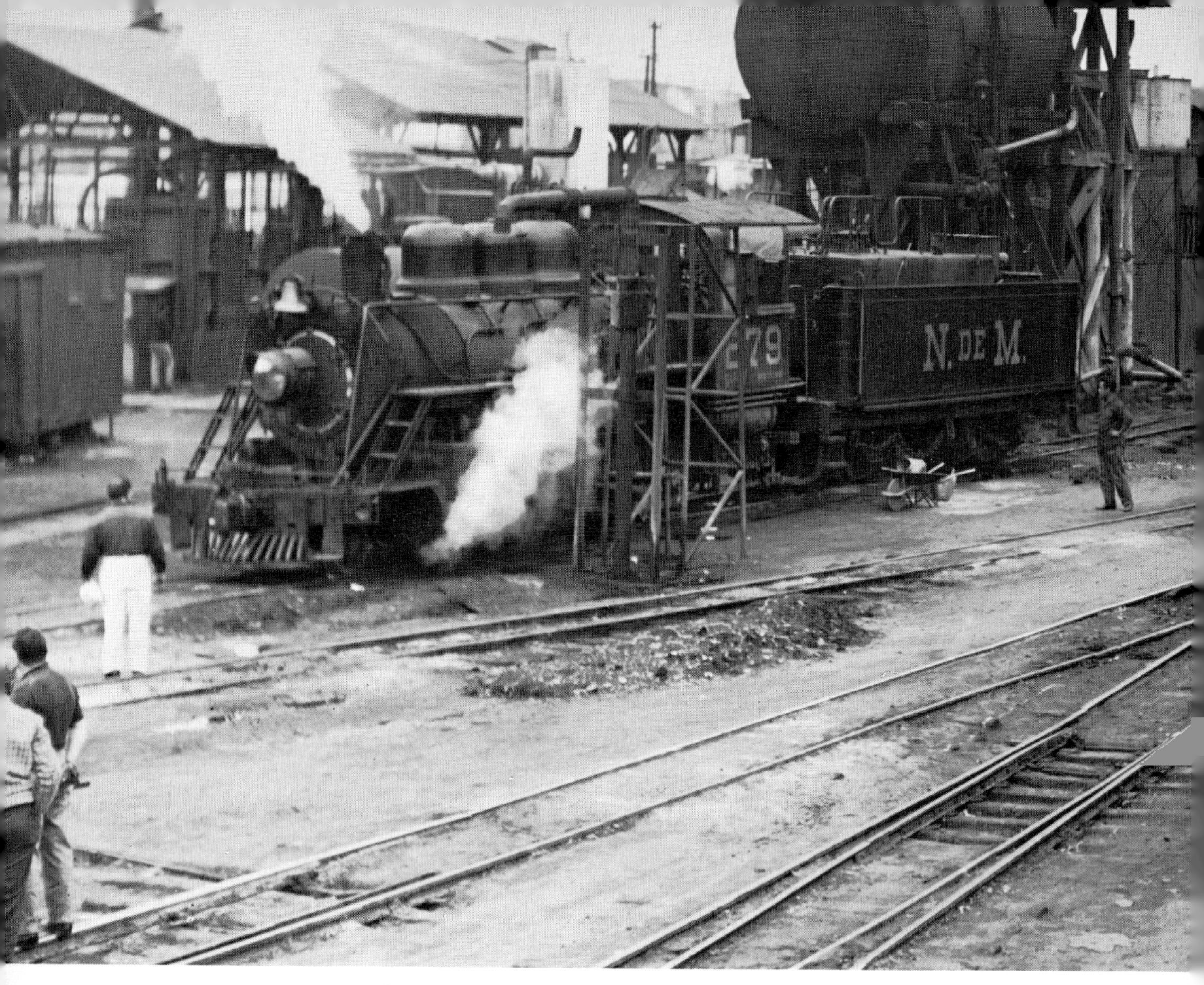

Operations in the primitive dual-gauge yard at San Lázaro, at the east end of Mexico

City, remained unchanged until the end of steam power. *Two photos, Ron Ziel*

Arrival at Amecameca
The arrival, in midafternoon, of the Ozumba local at Amecameca was a narrow-gauge thrill as late as 1966. Impatient passengers, *above,* detrain before the station as engine No. 262 pauses to quench her thirst at the big iron tank. A few minutes later the little 2-8-0 joins sister 279, *below,* and laborers load the express car. Consolidation No. 267 with a Mexico City-bound freight, *right,* pauses beyond a cistern which appeared bottomless. Even in 1964 trim ten-wheelers such as No. 185, *lower right,* still pulled passenger trains near Chalco.

Three photos, George H. Foster

Michael A. Eagleson

The Run to Ozumba

Before pulling a freight northward across the barren prairie toward Mexico City, two extra cars are filled with water, *below,* at Amecameca. The most photogenic location on the Cuautla branch was the bridge, *right,* just before Ozumba.

George H. Foster

José Dolorés Colunga

Three photos, George H. Foster

Mexican Meanderers
There are 328 miles of narrow-gauge track that carry passengers on a daily basis, down Mexico way, although the "growlers" are making their presence known rapidly. One passenger train rarely seen by outsiders is the afternoon accommodation from Puebla southward to Izúcar de Matamoros. On March 26, 1966, Consolidation No. 281, fresh from the shops, pulled this train, *right,* past a pair of tethered burros near Atlixco. The train to Ozumba leaves San Lázaro at 12:07 P.M. and makes the forty-two-mile run, returning, according to the timetable, at 4:55 P.M. The train is usually late but no one cares, for everyone seems to enjoy the ride. Here she is seen racing past an irrigation canal, *left,* pulled by No. 270. Passing through some of the most beautiful country in Mexico, two freights meet at Amecameca, which is situated at the foot of two extinct volcanoes, Popocatépetl and Ixtaccíhuatl. This photo was taken on the hill where is located the Santuario del Sacromonte (Shrine of the Sacred Mountain), which, next to the shrine of Guadalupe, is said to be the most venerated place in all Mexico.

Two photos, Ron Ziel

George H. Foster

The Lonely Little Pay Train
For years it was railroad practice to pay employees once or twice monthly. A special train with a pay car was sent to every branch in order to pay employees in cash. This practice was ended, for the most part, in the United States during the 1920's. Forty years later the N.deM. was still dispatching the pay car. On the narrow gauge it went out on the fifth and twentieth of every month. Having paid the employees at Los Reyes, the three-car extra, with soldiers decorating the boxcar, *left,* headed toward Amecameca. Goats seemed undisturbed by the lonely little train, *above,* which later paused at Ayotla, *upper left,* while section hands queued up for their *pesos,* and armed troops scrutinized the area.

George H. Foster

Mexico and Beyond

En route to Cuautla a freight, *above,* crosses a culvert on its southbound trek. The following evening the engine, No. 267, returned to Mexico City, *below,* with an extra comprised chiefly of stock cars. Central America, although physically a part of the North American continent, is generally grouped with the South American countries in such matters as geography, sociology, and transportation. Lines such as the Ferrocarril del Salvador were in steam during the 1960's and some outlived Mexican steam power. A 1918 American Locomotive Co. product, No. 35, is leaving Sitio del Niño, Salvador, *right,* on March 5, 1961.

Ron Ziel

Robert F. Collins

BURLINGT
RAILWAY EXPRESS
AGENCY

The Smoke That Was

The decade preceding 1960 was the period of dieselization on the railroads of North America. With the encroachment of the diesel, like a mighty fungus, there still remained several hundred engines listed on the rosters of class-one carriers, and hundreds more on short lines. Most of these had all but officially been retired and were being held either for preservation or a rise in scrap prices, depending on railroad managements. The Colorado & Southern's 2-8-0 No. 638, that road's last active steamer, was retired shortly after hauling a fan trip in Colorado on September 9, 1962.

Michael A. Eagleson

Colorado—The Last Stronghold

The Centennial State is known among rail historians for the Denver & Rio Grande Western narrow gauge—the last class-one steam operation in the United States. In the early sixties it still boasted more standard-gauge class-one steam power than virtually any other state. During the sugar-beet harvest season the Great Western fired up a few serviceable Consolidations and its famous 2-10-0. The last standard-gauge freight operation in steam, the Colorado & Southern's Climax spur kept a pair of 2-8-0's active through the early years of the sixties, and the Union Pacific and Burlington occasionally sent their last 4-8-4's into Colorado for fan trips. A narrow-gauge 2-8-0 at the Colorado Railroad Museum in Golden was fired up for special

Two photos, Ron Ziel

events, such as visiting fan groups. Later referred to as "The Last Great Steam Convention," the annual meeting of the National Railway Historical Society was held in Denver, under the auspices of the Intermountain Chapter, over Labor Day weekend in 1963. The Union Pacific and the Burlington Northerns were used, and Great Western trotted out the beloved decapod, No. 90, *upper left.* Although the Great Western was disposing of its 2-8-0's at the time, No. 90, the last operating 2-10-0 in North America, was held by the company. In June, 1962, Colorado & Southern, a subsidiary of the Burlington, ran a joint trip with the Great Western, *above,* as part of the annual Illini Club excursion to Colorado. Colorado & Southern 2-8-0 No. 638 and Great Western No. 90 powered separate segments of the memorable trip.

Three photos, Michael A. Eagleson

"Big Steam" Bows Out

To the Duluth, Missabe & Iron Range fell the distinction of closing out super-power steam operations in the United States. Only nominally a common carrier, the purpose of D.M.&I.R. was to keep the ever-hungry furnaces of its owner, United States Steel, supplied with iron ore. In this capacity it ran steam behemoths whose very wheel arrangements—2-8-8-4, 2-10-4, 2-10-2, 0-10-2—conjured up visions of the long trains they hauled from the rich pits in the Mesabi Mountains to the ore docks at Duluth. It was a far cry, indeed, from the nineteen-thousand-ton ore movements to a railfan excursion train one-fifteenth that weight as Yellowstone No. 224, *above*, struts her finest—and last—performance in Minnesota on July 2, 1961. The 569-ton engine, *right*, actually had a higher tractive force rating than Union Pacific's famed 4-8-8-4 Big Boys. After silencing the last 2-8-8-4, Missabe ran what was to be the last operating Santa Fe type, *upper right*, on September 2, 1962. The last active engine of monumental proportions not saved solely for fan service, No. 514, is battling Proctor Hill, Minnesota, with twelve cars of fans.

DULUTH MISSABE & IRON RANGE
224
112

Ron Ziel

Michael A. Eagleson

The Duluth & Northeastern

Among the last steam locomotives to drop their fires in the region of the Great Lakes were the 2-8-0's and 0-6-0's of Minnesota's Duluth & Northeastern. On September 2, 1962, Consolidations 14 and 27, *left*, put on a spectacular show for visiting rail photographers. A few months earlier 0-6-0 No. 29, a Lima War Department switcher built in 1944, *above*, shunted Northern Pacific boxcars. Both photos were taken at the Duluth & Northeastern yards in Cloquet. The 2-8-0's were bought secondhand from the Duluth, Missabe & Iron Range; the 0-6-0 was a standard U.S. Army type.

Karl R. Koenig

Ron Ziel

The Last Articulated Locomotives

The principle of articulation, which involved placing two sets of driving wheels and cylinders (engines) under one boiler, found wide acceptance on American railroads. Beginning with 0-6-6-0's at the turn of the century, and climaxing with such monsters as the 4-8-8-4's and 2-6-6-6's of the 1940's, over one thousand articulateds were built in America. The last of these to see service was a trio of relatively small 2-6-6-2 Mallets which were used to haul timber in the Pacific Northwest for the complex of logging roads belonging to Rayonier. Engine No. 38, *left*, which came from California's Little Sierra Railway, was photographed in March, 1963. As late as September of that year No. 111, *above*, an odd tank engine with a tender, could be seen in a heavy fog, switching log cars at the truck transfer near Hoquiam, Washington. Sister 110 and the popular 38 were still serviceable in early 1967, when negotiations were underway to move them cross-country to the Buffalo Creek & Gauley in West Virginia, whose revitalization was being planned.

A Tragic Abandonment

One of the finest and most fascinating operations in the latter days of steam was provided by two three-truck shays of the Klickitat Log & Lumber road owned by the St. Regis Paper Company, which operated out of Klickitat, Washington, near the Columbia River. The line featured stiff grades, big-time logging operations, spectacular scenery, and a tight horseshoe curve. During its final years the management, in a gesture of cooperation virtually unknown elsewhere, carried, free of charge, four passengers on the tank of the shay for the daylong journey. An old automobile seat provided rudimentary comforts, and the unique ride, for those fortunate enough to have taken it, proved to be a memorable experience. As one of the authors said, "Of all the steam roads, since abandoned, which I have traveled, if I could return to one, it would be the Klickitat." Approaching Wankiacus Crossing in 1961, *below,* Shay No. 7 brought a train of empties toward the reload. The inroads of progress were once again made when this wilderness gem was replaced. The Klickitat, with its two iron ribbons, was torn up and the tandem trailers now bring the logs to the mills. The last log train, with the fortunate few who rode that trip accommodated in a Pittsburgh & Lake Erie gondola, *left,* traversed the banks of the Klickitat River on April 3, 1964. The repugnant diesel trucks now defile this right-of-way where once the most beautiful of rustic short lines ran.

Two photos, Karl R. Koenig

Two photos, Ron Ziel

The Last in Their States

In the last years of steam it seemed that virtually every state in the Union contained one or two steam railroads. Then even the last ones disappeared. In September, 1963, shortly before the arrival of a diesel replacement, 2-6-2T No. 104 of the Peninsula Terminal, *above,* awaited switching assignments in Portland, Oregon. No sooner had 104 been sidelined than a new tourist road gave Oregon a reprieve from joining the list of states without steam. Running out of East Ely, the Nevada Northern's 1910 American Locomotive Co. 4-6-0 No. 40, *right,* was the last active steamer in the Silver State.

NEVADA NORTHERN
40

Workers to the End
Years after the steam power of the Minneapolis & St. Louis Railway had passed into oblivion, a half dozen of its 0-6-0's worked long drags of hoppers at the Midland Electric Coal Co. yard in Farmington, Illinois. On a cloudy day in August, 1963, No. 80, *right,* is seen moving a long cut of empties back toward the mines.

The Last C.B.&Q. Hog
For months after the Colorado & Southern ended freight operations behind steam, Burlington Mikado No. 4963, a duplicate of that road's famous excursion engine, the 4960, still switched coal hoppers at Bevier, Missouri. Along with No. 4943, the 1923 2-8-2 was leased to the coal-hauling Bevier & Southern, the last steam operation in Missouri. In August, 1962, No. 4963, *left*, brought a cut of loaded cars toward the C.B.&Q. interchange at Bevier.

Two photos, Ron Ziel

Three photos, Ron Ziel

A Few Hangers-on

Even as the Magma Copper Co. was searching for a diesel replacement for its handsome Baldwin 2-8-2 No. 7, this last active steamer in Arizona (along with 2-8-0 No. 5, which received a complete overhaul in the spring of 1967) continued to work the line from Superior to Magma Junction. On February 28, 1967, the Mikado took water at a sun-bleached tank, *above*, in the middle of the desert. Near Hewitt Station, *left*, No. 7 crossed many of the trestles which carry the tracks of the little railroad through desolate wasteland, unchanged since the last Apache war party passed the area eighty years ago. The Brimstone Railroad, an aptly named coal-moving shay operation, *upper right*, saw service in New River, Tennessee, as late as 1965. On a rainy day in January, 1962, the conductor and brakeman rode the pilot of 2-8-2 No. 10 of the Kentucky & Tennessee Railway, *right*, as she backed out of the yard at Stearns, Kentucky.

Michael A. Eagleson

Pride and Polish

The last surviving West Virginia short line in steam, the Buffalo Creek and Gauley, had a magnetic attraction for the faithful of the steam set during the early 1960's. Indeed, its three immaculately groomed Consolidations traversed the longest stretch of rail undefiled by traction motors east of the Mississippi River. From General Manager Richard Manning down, the policy was to operate big steam in microcosm and to welcome rail photographers. When the coal mine at Widen closed down in 1963, so did the railroad. America's most beautiful coal road was gone, and from Maine to the Carolina border revenue steam was extinct. Already in her last year of operation, 2-8-0 No. 4, *below,* unaware of impending disaster, switched the Baltimore & Ohio interchange at Dundon in January, 1963. Number 14 was the last of the trio under steam, *right,* in December of that year.

Two photos, Michael A. Eagleson

Will There Be an Encore?

Although the men of the Buffalo Creek & Gauley fought valiantly to turn the line into a tourist attraction, the owners decided to close it. Development of a rich new vein of coal just a few miles from Widen precluded the reopening of the railroad in 1967. 2-8-0 No. 13, *above,* had been sold, sisters 4 and 14 were scheduled to do lighter freight work and to pull excursion trains. The faithful anxiously awaited the resurrection but mourned the little shay at Swandale, *below,* which connected with the Buffalo Creek & Gauley, enhancing the wonders of the desolate West Virginia hills.

Three photos, Michael A. Eagleson

The Best Laid Schemes

In the summer of 1962 the Morehead & North Fork still employed 0-6-0 No. 12, *below*, but the diesels were only months away for the Kentucky short line. It was the avowed intention of the well-groomed and solvent Virginia Blue Ridge Railway to keep its stable of ex-U.S. Army 0-6-0's operating indefinitely. They stockpiled a ten-year supply of parts for that noble purpose, and the job of No. 9, *right*, seemed secure. Inexplicably diesels had bumped the five steamers by 1963, and they all headed north to round out the rosters of various tourist operations in New York, New Jersey, and Pennsylvania.

Ron Ziel

Michael A. Eagleson

Louisiana Gravel Engines

The gravel pits of Louisiana were a Siberia of sorts for cast-off steam locomotives. Even such handsome high-boilered machines as Ten-Wheeler No. 72, a 1928 Baldwin, *left,* suffered such an ignominious fate. Engines in this service were almost never viewed by the public and, being exempt from the usual government regulations, were invariably in scandalous mechanical condition. They were actually dangerous and frequently suffered boiler explosions and derailments. The Green Brothers Sand & Gravel Company at Franklinton, Louisiana, used many locomotives through the years, retiring No. 72 in 1964.

Two photos, Ron Ziel

Espee Steam in the Sixties

Few fans of the mighty Southern Pacific may have realized that two of its 0-6-0's were still in service ten years after the fires were dropped on the last of the great cab-forwards and the beautiful black and orange Daylight 4-8-4's. In fact, of the hundreds of steam locomotives condemned to the Siberia of the sandpits, S.P. No. 124, *above,* and sister 842, were the last active ones when Green Brothers retired them in July, 1966. The words "Southern Pacific" were still clearly visible on the tenders of the derelict six-wheelers—although upside down. When the tank developed multitudinous leaks the thoughtful shopmen simply flipped it over. The faded lettering, abundant rust, and S.P. stenciling which reads "Vacated 1954" are proof of the despicable maintenance of these engines—they had not even been painted since the original owner consigned them to scrap twelve years before.

Gone Away, Dixie Short Lines

The short lines of the South were the last redoubt of steam, even during the early 1960's. One of the more unusual operations was that of the Twin Seams Mining Company, *left,* at Kellerman, Alabama, whose affable old shay terminated the railroad's existence by falling through a bridge a few months after this photo was taken, in September, 1962. When Paulson Spence died in 1961 his collection of steam locomotives at Amite, Louisiana, *right,* was sold for scrap. Only the 4-4-0's, including No. 2, shown here under steam, were saved. His heirs could not see the value of the three Nickel Plate Hudsons and the thirty-odd other rarities in the priceless hoard. This, indeed, may have been the greatest single tragedy to befall steam during the sixties. Until she died of old age in 1964, No. 200 of the Willis Short Line, *below,* of Enon, Louisiana, was the oldest locomotive in revenue service in America—nearly eighty years. Leaking profusely, she had to pause in her laborious wanderings every few moments to build up steam.

Two photos, Ron Ziel

Wilbur T. Golson

Steam in Brooklyn

The Borough of Brooklyn in the City of New York has always been known for oddities—human, structural, natural, and mechanical. It was the logical place, then, to harbor the last revenue steam locomotives in the entire Northeast. Operating dead center in New York City, six heavy 0-6-0T's—five Porters, one Baldwin—held out against the diesels until 1963. After No. 10 was scrapped Nos. 12–16 carried on until dieselization of the Brooklyn Eastern District Terminal on October 25, 1963. The three Porters in the middle of the roster were Nos. 13, *right,* 14, *below* (alongside B.E.D.T. tugboat *Integrity*), and 15, *lower right,* shown during her last night under steam. The authors of this volume purchased Nos. 12 and 16; George Hart, operator of Rail Tours, acquired Nos. 13 and 14; and Ed Bernard, a New Jersey fan, plans to operate his investment, No. 15, on his own proposed length of trackage. It was a delightful anachronism during the 1960's to slip away to the edge of the East River and focus one's camera on a variety of saddle and side tankers, using the Empire State, Chrysler, and United Nations buildings for a background. Where else but in Brooklyn?

Three photos, Ron Ziel

B.E.D.T.
15

Short Lines

Once the class-one railroads had expelled steam power from their rosters, the short lines attained supreme interest from the faithful of the steam set. Although the smaller and somewhat unknown railroads of the land were rapidly dieselizing in the 1950's, their progress toward motive power monotony was somewhat slower and more practical than that of the larger roads which they fed. When a railroad decided to dieselize, the entire roster could change in a matter of months. The railroads, with their rapidly rising labor costs, found maintenance of double facilities an expense too large to be borne. This situation doomed many virtually new locomotives to the torch. A short line which possessed but two or three steam locomotives could run them almost until they fell apart before completing dieselization with the purchase or leasing of a secondhand diesel. Then, too, a steamer was often kept for years in standby service, to be called out only when its replacement was laid up for repairs. Consequently the only working steam locomotives to survive in the United States, as the 1970's loomed, were those frequently grimy, dank, comparatively small locomotives in short-line freight and industrial switching service. All of the others still operating were used for special excursion service and were responsible for nothing really useful in terms of serious railroading.

George H. Foster

Ron Ziel

A Goliath and Two Davids

The heaviest steam locomotives in regular service on American roads during the twilight of steam were of the 2-8-2 wheel arrangement. Mikado No. 31 of the Rockton & Rion, *left,* was one of these. Here, in the early light of a damp March morning in South Carolina, the Baldwin Mike seems to ooze steam from every pore as she is readied for her day's run from Anderson Quarry to the Southern Railway junction at Rockton. Also in the employ of the Rockton & Rion, 0-4-0T No. 1, built by the American Locomotive Company in 1913, earns her keep by pulling loads of stone, *above,* from the quarry. An equal to Rockton's No. 1 in terms of diminutive dimensions, the Edgmoor & Manetta's No. 5, *below,* is the sole steamer, beyond the trackage of the Rockton & Rion, to operate in South Carolina.

Michael A. Eagleson

Alabama's Iron Ponies

A little-known southern operation, even during the steam-starved sixties, was the T. R. Miller Mill Line at Brewton, Alabama. As late as April, 1966, an affable low-drivered Prairie, *above,* still switched the mill. Four years earlier a tank engine of 2-4-2 wheel arrangement, *below,* was one of the last of this unusual type, known as the Columbia, to run in the United States. T. R. Miller used it in standby service. The Calcasieu Paper Company maintained swivel-headlighted 2-6-2 No. 107, *right,* and a similar sister in service into the mid-1960's at its large mill near Elizabeth, Louisiana.

Three photos, Wilbur T. Golson

Wilbur T. Golson

Mississippi Holdout

When the Bonhomie & Hattiesburg Southern retired its 2-6-2 and 2-8-2 in 1961, only the Mississippian Railway remained to keep that state represented by steam. Years later its two ex-Frisco Consolidations, Nos. 76, *above*, and 77, *below*, were still very active between Fulton and Amory. On the return trip from Fulton No. 77, *right*, shuffles through a late afternoon in March, 1966, near Tilden.

Two photos, George H. Foster

Three photos, Wilbur T. Golson

The Crowning Irony

Probably the quaintest little railway operations in the world were the narrow-gauge plantation locomotives which ran in the Philippines, Indonesia, the Caribbean, and Central America. Incredibly they had a counterpart in the Westfield Sugar Company line which ran at Paincourtville, Louisiana, until 1963. *Left,* 0-4-4T No. 3 and 0-6-2T No. 1, *above,* both built by Porter, switched four-wheel cane cars. These cane cars were throwbacks to the early days of railroading, still utilizing the primitive practice of link-and-pin coupling. Number 3 is crossing standard-gauge Texas & Pacific trackage, another circumstance quite rare even at the peak of narrow-gauge operations seventy years earlier. As if the survival of these ancient methods and locomotives was not enough, the 2-6-2, *below,* is indeed bewildering. By the end of 1966 this engine, in the employ of the Louisiana Longleaf Lumber Company at Fisher, was not only the last operating steamer in the state, she was also the last wood burner used in active service on the continent!

Ron Ziel

George H. Foster

The Three R's

As steam on the cherished short lines disappeared in the sixties, the remaining steam lines gained an almost mystic aura of historical importance. Certainly the Rockton & Rion Railway in South Carolina was the epitome of steam power during this era. Every operating day found two engines under steam. The locomotives were delightful amalgamations of soot and rust which contrasted sharply with the light stone that was the freight of their existence. There was a red-clay cut, *left,* surmounted by a bridge, which afforded a view that was impressive from any angle. And the friendly Negro engine crew, a rarity not peculiar to Dixie, obliged visiting photographers with the blackest soft-coal smoke imaginable, as demonstrated by No. 19, a 1906 Baldwin, *above,* in September, 1965.

Three photos, Ron Ziel

Eat 'Taters & Wear No Clothes

The East Tennessee & Western North Carolina Railway was renowned, long before the demise of steam, because of its beloved narrow-gauge operations, which were affectionately called "Tweetsie" by the local mountain folk. For years two Consolidations, formerly the property of the Southern Railway, worked the nine miles of standard-gauge track between Johnson City and Elizabethtown, Tennessee. By 1965 these two spotlessly maintained sixty-year-old 2-8-0's had become the last active steam locomotives in the state. Their latter-day fame notwithstanding, Nos. 207 and 208, shown here at Elizabethton in September, 1965, and March, 1966, worked hard. The busy little railroad had come upon happy days which may well have been envied by the class-one carriers whose cars they moved. In January, 1962, two shopmen, *below*, adjusted the shining valve gear of No. 208.

1926
F

Two photos, Ron Ziel

Carolina and Alabama

The fame of North Carolina's last steam operation, the shays of the Graham County Railroad, had spread too far to resist the temptation of attracting the tourists who are the mainstay of the Cherokee region. In the spring of 1966 the Graham County Railroad acquired two more shays, gave Nos. 1925 and 1926, *left,* new paint jobs, erected some nondescript open excursion cars on old flats, built a tourist center known as Bear Creek Junction, and went to work hauling passengers while continuing its freight operations. Much of the backwoods charm was lost in the process, but the continuance of the Graham County Railroad in steam was assured. As author Ron Ziel focused his fifty-eight-year-old 5-inch by 7-inch Press Graflex on Engineer Clive Kundrick, *right,* Alabama's last active steamer, Mogul No. 97, *above,* simmered in the background, waiting to perform the day's switching at the Brownville yard.

George H. Foster

Little Workers

The Ely Thomas Lumber Company's tired old shay No. 2, with boxcar in tow, *below*, puttered about stacks of lumber in Fenwick, West Virginia, on a rainy September 13, 1965. Shortly thereafter she was retired from active service and went north to Pennsylvania to join the Strasburg Rail Road. By the winter of 1965 the only steam engine to see occasional useful service in the entire state of Texas was Angelina & Neches River 2-8-2 No. 110, *right*, at Herty, Texas, where she met the Southern Pacific. An ex-Illinois Central 0-8-0, No. 3566, *lower right*, switched hoppers during an Alabama winter for the De Bardeleben Coal Corporation at Holt.

Ron Ziel

Michael A. Eagleson

Wilbur T. Golson

Two photos, Ron Ziel

Steam Spectacular—Military Style

The United States Army Transportation Corps post at Fort Eustis, near Norfolk, Virginia, is the only place in the country where men are still formally trained in the maintenance and operation of steam locomotives. A half-dozen War Department 2-8-0's are serviceable, and No. 611, *above,* is the only poppet-valve engine operating in the United States. During the National Railway Historical Society Convention in Richmond over the 1966 Labor Day holiday, the Army ran what was probably the most spectacular fan trip in a decade. Instead of supplying two locomotives for the N.R.H.S. Special, as planned, a triple-header, *right,* consisting of G.I. Consolidations Nos. 612 and 611 (Baldwin, 1943) and No. 606 (Lima, 1945), barked up a tumultuous crescendo to the delight of more than seven hundred railfans who were fortunate enough to be at Fort Eustis on that bright September 3.

UNITED STATES ARMY
612
612

Michael A. Eagleson

Reprieve from the Torch

During a ten-year period ending in 1965 the Northwestern Steel & Wire Company at Sterling, Illinois, cut up nearly one thousand steam locomotives and fed their mangled remains into the mill's huge electric process smelters. Because Northwestern had a choice roster of modern discards to choose from, it has become the last bastion of steam in Illinois. Here nearly a dozen big Grand Trunk Western 0-8-0's (the last of their wheel arrangement in service) are rotated in switching duties; three or four are kept fired up at all times. Number 06 (ex-G.T.W. No. 8306) switches at the mill which consumed many of her sisters, *left*, while No. 79 (ex-G.T.W. 8379) takes on coal, *below*, between chores.

Ron Ziel

Ron Ziel

Wilbur T. Golson

Arizona Copper Road

The Magma Copper Company in Superior, Arizona, uses a large 2-8-0 and a small 2-8-2 which are still in freight service. The locomotives were well groomed and quite handsome as they moved freight drags from the Southern Pacific interchange at Magma to the copper smelter in Superior, twenty-eight miles across the desert. Probably the most endearing feature of the Magma Arizona engines was the shiny copper color of their smokeboxes, a beautiful departure from the customary graphite coating. The company had developed a copper-base paint especially for use on its locomotives. On a September morning in 1962 Mikado No. 7, *left,* leaves the enginehouse at Superior, while Consolidation No. 5 rests in the adjoining stall. Several years later No. 5, *above,* switched ore cars at Globe.

Three photos, Karl R. Koenig

Pacific Coast Steam

The Pickering Lumber Company had one of the last steam logging roads in California. In 1962 Shay No. 33, *above,* moved a work train at Lyons, California. On October 25, 1966, the division of Fibreboard Paper Company ran a Directors' Special to acquaint management with a proposed tourist operation over its standard-gauge trackage between Standard and Lyons Dam. By 1964 Vancouver Plywood Heisler No. 2, *below,* sat forlornly out of service on a forgotten siding in Mill City, Oregon. On June 1, 1963, the Feather River Railway fired up Shays Nos. 2 and 3, *right,* to give a fan group quite a ride in excursion cars which resembled first-class accommodations for cattle. From all accounts they had a joyous time on that California spring day.

Two photos, Karl R. Koenig

On Location—with Steam

When Hollywood needs a vintage steam locomotive for Western thrillers, it is apt to turn to the Sierra Railroad at Jamestown, California. Heading for a film assignment in *The Great Race, above,* in 1965, is 4-6-0 No. 3. When dressed up in a balloon stack and fancy paint, the ten-wheeler is known to millions of television viewers as the *Hooterville Cannonball* on "Petticoat Junction." *Right,* 2-8-0 No. 28 is running near Tuolumne with a fan trip in 1962.

28

Two photos, Karl R. Koenig

Tank Engines East and West

Howard Terminal Railway 2-6-2T No. 6, *above,* was still switching the docks at Oakland, California, in 1960. The 1922 Baldwin, formerly Sierra Railroad No. 30, is now owned by the Pacific Locomotive Association. Quincy Railroad side tanker No. 2, *right,* moved a Western Pacific gondola over the Quincy River bridge in 1962. The California short line has also hauled excursion trains. April 9, 1967, found E. J. Lavino 0-6-0 No. 5, *upper right,* switching that company's big complex at Lynchburg, Virginia.

Michael A. Eagleson

29
CANADI

Maple Leaves and Beavers

The year 1960 saw the complete dieselization of the Canadian Pacific Railway, only months after the Canadian National had dropped the fires. Like United States roads, however, the Canadian carriers had quite a few serviceable steam locomotives on hand, and for a while at least, a variety of them were available to pull excursion trains. The most startling engine of all was a little 4-4-0, built around 1887, which had been in branch-line service with two other vintage Americans right until the diesels came. The fact that No. 29 was still operable in 1960 lent an air of incredibility to the trips she pulled through the Province of Quebec. Elsewhere the boilers of Royal Hudsons, Consolidations, ten-wheelers, Selkirks, Mountains, Moguls, and six- and eight-wheel switchers were all cold on the two great Canadian carriers months before. The last Pacific ran in 1962, and a few cast-off 2-6-0's and 2-8-0's could be found in private industrial yards. A brace of geared engines survived in British Columbia until the end of the 1960's. But on the main line it was just one C.N.R. 4-8-4 which prevented Canada from becoming 100 percent dieselized.

An American in Quebec
Rushing across hayfields after the autumn harvest, Canadian Pacific No. 29, a seventy-three-year-old 4-4-0, pulls her last train, a Canadian Railway Historical Association extra, in October, 1960. This study of the last American type to see regular service on a class-one railroad in North America was taken by Victor Hand, one of the most talented photographers to stalk steam power in the 1960's; he was eighteen at the time. Here No. 29 steams her last near St. Lin, after a long, useful existence which began in 1887.

Donald S. Robinson

Two photos, Vincent Alvino

In the Last Days

During the early winter of 1960 steam made its last stand in Quebec, even as the final units of a massive diesel order were being erected and made ready for delivery. Unlike most United States locomotives in their last days, the C.P.R. Consolidations, ten-wheelers, and Pacifics which wrote finis to the final chapter of big steam in Anglo-Saxon North America were maintained in presentable condition right until the end. C.P.R.-subsidiary Quebec Central 4-6-2 No. 2556 crossed a trestle near Eaton Corner, Quebec, *left,* on January 15, 1960. Decrepit old 4-6-0 No. 425, *lower right,* one of the last of C.P.R.'s affable old 4-6-0's, is being turned at Ottawa in steam's final hour. One of C.P.R.'s big Pacifics, No. 2334, is shown in St. Luc yard, in the company of 2-8-0 No. 3642, *lower left,* after the pair double-headed a freight into Montreal, in the last year of steam.

With the Snows of Yesteryear

Two of Canadian Pacific's handsome Royal Hudson 4-6-4's, Nos. 2825 and 2822, are shown in their last month of operation, at Westmount, a suburb of Montreal. These locomotives, of the same class that pulled the 1939 royal train in Canada, were named Royal Hudsons, with his Majesty's permission. Except for a few Hudsons in Mexico, these 2800's were the last 4-6-4's to run on the continent which developed that classic wheel arrangement. These pictures were taken in February, 1960, when the end of steam on Canadian rails was only days away. Plying a branch north of Ottawa, ten-wheeler No. 425, *right,* switches near a water tank.

Two photos, Michael A. Eagleson

Vincent Alvino

The End of an Era—Almost

When Canadian National retired the last engine on its roster of serviceable steam power in October, 1961, No. 6153 was rolled into Turcot roundhouse in Montreal and two officials closed the doors behind her. Happily the retirement was premature, for she was back under steam the following year, when she pulled fan trips in tandem with Pacific No. 5107. This photographic nocturne, *lower right,* is at the Montreal shops on June 23, 1962, getting ready for action at Charette, Quebec, the next day. A Royal Hudson, *below,* shuffled through Glen yard, Westmount, in 1960.

Three photos, Michael A. Eagleson

5107
12
10
8

6167
6167

Double-heading Northerns

For the first half of the 1960's the most famous locomotive in Canada was C.N.R. 4-8-4 No. 6167, which drew most of the fan-trip assignments. When she became due for a major overhaul, a later member of the U-2 class, No. 6218, was put through the shops. On September 27, 1964, a doubleheader was run just prior to the retirement of 6167. With the outgoing 4-8-4 in the lead, the eleven-car excursion is shown at Dundas, *left,* Mount Hope, *lower left,* and Cainsville, *below,* all in the Province of Ontario.

Three photos, Michael A. Eagleson

Two photos, Ron Ziel

Nomadic Northerns

On January 27, 1963, No. 6167, *right,* roared through a daylong blizzard providing the fortunate photographers aboard ample opportunities to recall Canadian winter steam operations in the grand manner during five photo run-pasts. As the sixties wore on, the 6218 gained fame far beyond the subdivisions radiating from Montreal and Toronto where she normally worked, *above.* Several times she skipped across the border on forays into New England, traveling on the tracks of the Central Vermont, Grand Trunk, Boston & Maine, and the New Haven. She got as far south as New London and Groton, Connecticut, on Long Island Sound. In her ever-expanding role the 6218 has even operated on the Grand Trunk Western in Michigan. Semistreamlined Pacifics Nos. 2408 and 2412, *below,* are on the Glen yard ready track in their last week of service in 1960.

Michael A. Eagleson

6167 6167
CANADIAN
6167
NATIONAL

Two photos, Ron Ziel

The Last of Canadian Steam

Late in the decade of the 1960's the 6218 could be found winter and summer, *opposite page*, filling a long schedule of fan-trip assignments. The dearth of industrial and switching roads in Canada left far fewer short-line engines operating in the Dominion than could be found in the United States. Among those were Hillcrest Lumber Ltd.'s famous Climax, *right*, the last of those geared engines in regular service. She was built in 1915 and operated at the Mesachie Lake mill in British Columbia. The last steam engine in Nova Scotia, 2-6-0 No. 17, *below*, joined over a hundred other preserved Canadian locomotives which were in museums by the end of 1967.

Wilbur T. Golson

Daniel A. Foley

For Fun and Profit

As the steam locomotive was being purged from railroading there arose groups of concerned historians who clamored for the preservation of representative types of engines. Not content with having locomotives statically displayed in parks, the do-it-yourself railroaders, frequently under the guidance of professional railroad men, now account for most of the steam train-miles.

Frequently nonprofit operating railway museums run steam trains on weekends and holidays during the pleasant months. The operators of most tourist railroads enjoy the excitement, the hustle and bustle of their operation, from the smoke and cinders to the smiles and squeaks of pleasure from little children. The history of the Great Iron Horse takes the form of reality in a way no mundane textbook ever could. A few common carriers have acquired or returned inactive steamers to service to haul passenger extras and, perhaps, occasional freights. Other tourist lines have been established on abandoned trackage or in entirely new locations as profitable enterprises. They are generally quite successful and often become the major tourist attractions in their regions.

The number of fan-and-tourist-attraction locomotives has increased proportionately to the engines retired. In fact, it is not uncommon for a locomotive to be sold by a common carrier and run under its own power to one of the new passenger roads, where it is immediately ready to work. Such were the cases of Strasburg's Camelback and Cass's Heisler. This was the big steam story in the sixties: the transition of steam power from its traditional operating role to that of an amusement attraction.

George H. Foster

Ron Ziel

George H. Foster

The Hawk Mountain Line

One of the new steam lines which has made Pennsylvania The Steam State in the 1960's is the Wanamaker, Kempton & Southern, which owns an ex-Reading branch between the two towns of its corporate title. The station at Kempton, *left,* is seen from the interior of an old wooden coach which houses a museum of railroadiana. In addition to two saddle-tank engines, the W., K. & S. operates a large, comparatively handsome 2-6-2, *above,* which was purchased from Mississippi's Bonhomie & Hattiesburg Southern. William Whitehead, *right,* founder of a similar line, the Black River & Western, on a busman's holiday, pays a visit to the Wanamaker, Kempton & Southern.

Two photos, Michael A. Eagleson

Immigrants from the South and West

With the choice locomotives gone from most regions, prospective steam railroads had to go far afield to find suitable motive power for their purposes. The Black River & Western, which is centered in the flourishing tourist area along the Delaware River in western New Jersey, was fortunate to obtain a handsome Consolidation, *below,* from the Great Western in Colorado. Also on the roster, a Delaware, Lackawanna & Western Mogul, *above,* was fired up in 1960. This was the last D.L.&W. steam engine to operate. Up in the Finger Lakes region of New York State, the Livonia, Avon & Lakeville, a common-carrier freight road, uses the trim Mikado, *right,* for dual service during the summer months. The engine, originally operating on the Savannah & Atlanta Railway in Georgia, went to West Virginia's Buffalo Creek & Gauley before its final trip north. Unfortunately the appearance of the engine belies the claim that she has been "meticulously restored." She once sported a formidable feedwater heater forward of the stack in a manner virtually vanquished from existing steam engines. For an inexplicable reason the heater was replaced with an awkward bell mounting, destroying much of the individuality of the 2-8-2.

George H. Foster

12
15
E. B.

The Last Eastern Narrow Gauge

The steam revival has put a stigma on the narrow-gauge heritage, which was one of the most enchanting aspects of railroading. Narrow-gauge lines came into being because they were more economical to construct and operate than standard gauge. In the hapless drift toward mediocrity and cheap sensationalism, the promoters of tasteless tourist roads turned to three-foot gauge for the same reason. Because of this, some standard-gauge lines even advertise the fact that they are not a tourist trap "or a narrow gauge." The East Broad Top, in central Pennsylvania, is the only genuine narrow gauge east of the Mississippi River, all the rest having been abandoned. After seeing the monstrous travesties which bill themselves as "narrow-gauge railroads" prevalent in the Smoky Mountains and the South, the businesslike manner in which the East Broad Top operates its three 2-8-2's is a welcome relief. Number 12, *left,* traverses the narrow-gauge iron, originally laid in 1874, en route to Shirleysburg from the shops and main terminal at Orbisonia. Numbers 12 and 15, *below,* switch the yard at Orbisonia.

Two photos, Ron Ziel

92

Steam Returns to Delaware
In 1966 a nonprofit corporation, the Historic Red Clay Valley, Inc., began running steam trips over the Baltimore & Ohio's Landenberg branch on weekends. Having acquired the ideal motive power for a short-haul steam road—a 2-6-0 Mogul and a 4-4-0 American—the corporation tied the steam trains in with a comprehensive plan to promote the historical attractions of the Red Clay Creek Valley. There is an old mill, covered bridges, and plans for attractive recreational facilities to complement the historical complex. The railroad is a professional operation, the equipment is generally tasteful in restoration, and the name, Wilmington & Western, is a re-creation of the original railroad built in 1872 and purchased by the Baltimore & Ohio in 1883. Because of coordinated regional planning, an awareness of its assets and liabilities, and dedicated labor by reliable volunteers, the Wilmington & Western stands to become a model of serious historical preservation. Ex-Canadian National 2-6-0 No. 92, *left,* crosses Red Clay Creek during an October rainstorm. Author George H. Foster discusses operations with Wilmington & Western General Manager (and Conductor) Thomas C. Marshall, *right,* while passengers, *below,* disembark from the coaches at Greenbank Station on Route 41, west of Wilmington.

Robert L. Havens

Two photos, George H. Foster

Weedy and Wonderful

The Empire State Railway Museum runs Sundays on trackage of the Middletown & New Jersey Railroad. *Below,* 2-6-2 No. 103 pulls these trains south from Middletown, New York, along a scenic right-of-way. The New Hope & Ivyland, a common carrier which works its ex-Canadian National ten-wheeler, No. 1533, on freight details throughout the year, is one of the few steamers left which performs in a winter setting. After the tourist season ends she is allowed to deteriorate to a delightfully shabby, rusty, hard-working appearance. During the winter of 1967 the 4-6-0, *right,* looked as if she had returned to her native Dominion haunts when steam still ruled all the little branch lines of the once-glorious Canadian National Railways.

Ron Ziel

Michael A. Eagleson

1533
NEW HOPE
1533
& IVYLAND
NEW HOPE

Two photos, Ron Ziel

Steam in Morris County

One railfan group, after seven years of work, returned steam to New Jersey in 1965. Having acquired an ex-Virginia Blue Ridge, ex-Southern 2-8-0, *above,* the Morris County Central runs a good operation through the woodlands of suburban New Jersey. In 1966 another ex-Virginia Blue Ridge locomotive, a U.S. Army-designed 0-6-0, *right,* led the Consolidation on double-headed excursions out of Morristown. The Morris County Central is a good example of what a conscientious group can accomplish, with moderate resources and good taste, in the preservation of operating steam.

MORRIS COUNTY CENTRAL
4039
4039

George H. Foster

Michael A. Eagleson

The Arcade & Attica

Early in the 1960's the Arcade & Attica, a short-line freight road southeast of Buffalo, New York, was operating deep in the red and might well have been closed. Then the management acquired two steam locomotives, put them in passenger service, and within two years stockholders, who had long before given up on the value of their holdings, received a dividend for the first time in their memory. Ten-wheeler No. 14, shown here leaving Arcade en route to the terminal of passenger service at Curriers, is the principal locomotive used to carry the families and groups of schoolchildren over the line. Diesels still handle the freight service which is interchanged with the Pennsylvania Railroad at Arcade.

14
ARCADE & ATTICA

18

Two photos, Ron Ziel

Orange and Black among the Green and Gray

While the Arcade & Attica is a fine operation, professional in most ways, its unfortunate choice of orange and black as company colors has led some cynical purists to call the line the Halloween Central. Orange is a difficult color to use tastefully, particularly with a neutral color such as black, white, or gray (as Long Island Rail Road riders have learned from that line's current unattractive orange and "prison gray" scheme). Only the Southern Pacific, by retaining the services of prominent industrial designers, came up with a beautiful combination of orange and black offset by white and red for their Daylight trains in the late thirties. The huge circuslike lettering on the coaches, *below*, does not help the image. Numbers 14 and 18, *left*, were both fired up on August 24, 1966, a rare circumstance prompted by the authors' visit. Rolling through the plush green pastures of the New York dairy land, *above*, No. 18 brings a train into Curriers, her bell at a jaunty swing. The heavy gray clouds are typical of the weather in western New York and give a dramatic background to the little steam trains.

George H. Foster

Michael A. Eagleson

Coal Smoke over the Alleghenies

The Cass Scenic Railroad, owned by the state of West Virginia, is one of the most spectacular tourist lines, operating a trio of shays and a Heisler. The road is extremely cooperative with rail enthusiasts, frequently operating special doubleheaders, with the engines pulling in front instead of their normal pusher position, *above*. On December 12–14, 1966, the Cass moved Heisler No. 6, newly acquired from the Meadow River Lumber Company at Rainelle, over more than a hundred miles of Chesapeake & Ohio main line. December 13 saw the Heisler churning through a heavy snowfall, *below*, near Bellwood. The next day she ran past the last operable watering facility on the Chesapeake & Ohio branch, *left*, at Marlinton. The Cass management set an excellent precedent by informing interested photographers of the pending move several weeks earlier.

Two photos, Ron Ziel

George H. Foster

Big Steam on a Shoestring

Of the few steam operations which are well run, use historically accurate equipment, and consider the desires of the passengers, none is superior to that of Rail Tours, Inc., headquartered at York, Pennsylvania. Railfan George Hart, owner of six locomotives, runs weekend trips over the Maryland & Pennsylvania Railroad (the "Ma & Pa" of past glories in steam) to Yoe and Red Lion in the Amish country. He is just as likely to extend the journey through bucolic backwoods to Delta, on the Maryland border. Sometimes these trips are made in the light of a full moon, with kerosene or arc lights supplying a minimum of interior illumination. The most spectacular trips, however, are sixty-miles-per-hour doubleheaders on the high iron of the Western Maryland, such as the run of October 22, 1966, *right,* with an ex-Canadian Pacific 4-6-2 and 4-6-0 approaching Gettysburg, Pennsylvania, en route to Cumberland, Maryland. Reflected in a coach window, *above,* a mechanic adjusts the spark arrester on No. 972's stack, while Hart, *below* (with glasses), surveys his coaling operation.

George H. Foster

Ron Ziel

1286

George H. Foster

Two photos, Ron Ziel

A Kaleidoscope of Power

Although George Hart purchased all of his six-coupled locomotives (two C.P.R. 4-6-2's, one C.P.R. 4-6-0, two B.E.D.T. 0-6-0T's, one Reading 0-6-0T), he has retained the original paint schemes on all of them, and the "Canadian Pacific" lettering on the C.P.R. power. The Ma & Pa is still in possession of such antiquities as the hand-operated turntable at Delta, *upper left,* and the picturesque wooden trestles near Red Lion, *left,* plus charming little towns and a few ramshackle abandoned stations. Farmland, heavily forested hills, factory yards—all are to be found along the many curves of the Ma & Pa, and make for photographs reminiscent of the days when steam was everywhere. A half hour after midnight on August 28, 1966, ten-wheeler No. 972, *above,* paused on a moonlit excursion near Delta. Such journeys, so common two generations ago, are a truly wonderful experience and are among the rarest of occurrences in the 1960's.

Along the Ma & Pa

The Canadian Pacific ten-wheeler which is the mainstay of the Rail Tours operations exchanges close-up looks with her admirers in an ex-C.P.R. excursion car as she returns to York from a Sunday trip to Red Lion. A lack of turning facilities at the latter station necessitates running backward for half the trip.

George H. Foster

Gold Coast Railroad

The Miami Railway Historical Society has moved the entire Gold Coast Railroad to Fort Lauderdale, where it now operates passenger trips along the waterfront. Their little Florida East Coast Railway Pacific, No. 153, shown here, ran on the south campus of the University of Miami for many years.

Ron Ziel

Wilbur T. Golson

SYLVANIA
1223

Two photos, Ron Ziel

"The Road to Paradise"

With the passing years the Strasburg Railroad, which operates between Strasburg and Paradise, Pennsylvania, has become the best known and most widely patronized of the serious steam tourist lines. Although a common carrier, the Strasburg derives the vast majority of its revenue from passengers. The little line runs right through the heart of the Pennsylvania Dutch farmland east of Lancaster, and in just a few years has become the biggest tourist attraction in an area already known for such things. By 1966 the Strasburg was carrying over 225,000 passengers annually, without resorting to such inanities as "Indian attacks" or bright yellow paint. The biggest steam news of the mid-sixties was the tentative plan of the Pennsylvania State Historical Society to locate most of the locomotives and antique equipment preserved by the Pennsylvania Railroad on the Strasburg. Already the Strasburg had refurbished and was running D-16sb No. 1223, *left*, in regular service. The Strasburg's original engine, ex-Canadian National 0-6-0 No. 7312 (renumbered 31), pulled a passenger train, *above*, past the D-16sb-powered Board of Directors Special at Strasburg on September 11, 1965.

STRASBURG
4
RAIL-ROAD
4

Last of the Breed

The wide Wooten fireboxes necessitated by the burning of anthracite coal resulted in many locomotives having been built with their cabs astride the boiler to allow the engineer better visibility. Known commonly as Camelbacks, or Mother Hubbards, the center-cab locomotives were mostly retired long before dieselization. Consequently only one is preserved in running condition, with just two others in museums. The Strasburg Railroad acquired a Baldwin 0-4-0 Camelback, built for the Reading in 1903, from the Colorado Fuel & Iron Company, in Birdsboro, Pennsylvania. Historically one of the most important locomotives under steam, No. 4 is shown, in 1963, bringing an eight-car train down the main line toward the rural community of Strasburg.

Michael A. Eagleson

Two photos, Donald S. Robinson

Wooden Trestles for the Tourists

Probably the oldest tourist railroad in the world (almost one hundred years), the Mount Washington Cog Railway is still powered by odd little nineteenth-century steam engines, *above.* For five generations this line, employing a gearing system which engages a ratchet between the running rails to prevent the trains from slipping down the 25 percent grades, has been one of New Hampshire's most popular attractions. One of the few tourist railways in Canada, the Cowichan Valley, *right,* is part of a logging museum at Duncan, British Columbia. A two-truck shay, built by Lima in 1920, serves as the principal motive power to pull carloads of passengers around an oval track less than a mile in length. The restoration job is serious, and the equipment has been refurbished to its original appearance.

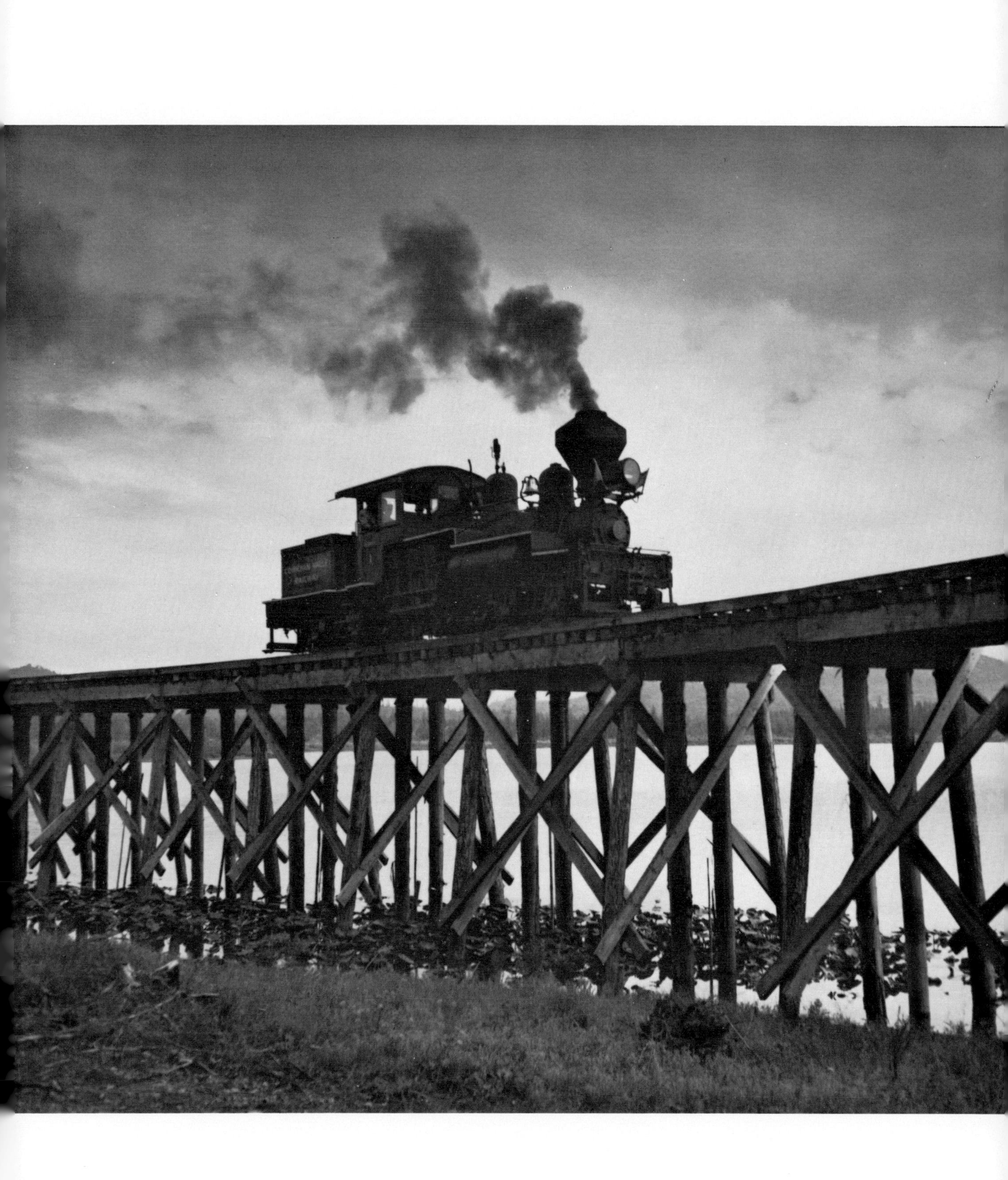

A Steam Railroad for Long Island

Among the many projected operating steam lines in the late sixties was the Sag Harbor & Scuttle Hole Rail Road in the exclusive Hamptons, on Long Island's South Shore. Planned by the authors of this narrative, the S.H.&S.H. was to run from a junction with the Long Island Rail Road at Bridgehampton (ninety-four miles east of New York City) to the famed historical whaling port of Sag Harbor, on an abandoned right-of-way which was originally built in 1870. Scuttle Hole, a nearby farming community, was to lend its name to a projected 1910-era village, and it was planned that an excursion bus would meet trains at Sag Harbor and carry passengers on tours of the town and its many historical sites. Four years of preliminary work included the purchase, by the authors, of Brooklyn Eastern District Terminal 0-6-0 tank engines Nos. 12, *right*, and 16, *below*, as well as tons of spare parts, antique signals, and other equipment. By 1967 a general office had been opened in Bridgehampton, the right-of-way was spoken for, and one of America's most beautiful private open observation cars had been leased. When the S.H.&S.H. moved a large wooden nineteen-thousand-series New York Central caboose out to the East End, the Long Island Rail Road welcomed it onto its rails. While NBC-TV cameramen and news photographers recorded the event, L.I.R.R. President Thomas M. Goodfellow now head of Association of American Railroads, inspected the 1895-design way car. *Below right*, Paul Carey, assistant to S.H.&S.H. President, and owner of the car; George H. Foster, S.H.&S.H. President; Thomas M. Goodfellow and Ron Ziel, S.H.&S.H. General Manager. Other equipment, including larger locomotives, was being negotiated for. The Sag Harbor & Scuttle Hole Rail Road, connecting with passenger trains of the L.I.R.R. on one end, and accessible by pleasure boats on the other, promised to become the major historical attraction and a haven for vacationers who found relatively few amusements in an area of boundless natural beauty which attracts millions of visitors annually.

F. G. Zahn

Ron Ziel

Richard Glueck

Karl R. Koenig

H. F. Stewart

Ron Ziel

Tourist Lines Far Apart

Arizona acquired an excursion line with the opening of the White Mountain Scenic Railroad at McNary. Number 100, an ex-Santa Maria Valley 2-8-2, *above,* is en route to Apache Springs from McNary on June 10, 1966. Sierra Railroad Mikado No. 36, *left,* was fired up for inspection at Jamestown, California, in 1965, prior to her movement to McNary. The Connecticut Valley Chapter of the N.R.H.S. maintains a fine traction museum at Warehouse Point, Connecticut. In addition to the antique trolley cars, the museum operates an 0-4-0 tank engine, No. 5, *above,* for the benefit of its members and visitors.

346
RIO GRANDE SOUTHERN
0404

Three photos, Ron Ziel

Standard, Narrow, and Miniature

The Colorado Railroad Museum at Golden operates its historical Rio Grande narrow-gauge 2-8-0, *above left*, on special occasions. Such a time occurred during the 1963 N.R.H.S. Convention when, on August 30, one of Burlington's celebrated 4-8-4's, No. 5629, *left*, was put on permanent display at the museum. The beautiful miniature 4-4-2 Atlantic, *above*, is the pride of the Sandley Light Railway in Wisconsin Dells, Wisconsin. Owner Norman Sandley maintains a complete shop and crew of skilled craftsmen who build engines such as No. 128 completely from scratch, at a cost higher than the standard-gauge prototype cost at Baldwin in 1910.

476
Rio Grande

Steeped in History

The term "historical preservation," so often associated with steam in the sixties, can scarcely do justice to the Silverton branch of the Denver & Rio Grande Western narrow gauge, constructed only five years after Colorado's admission to the Union in 1876. This line served as an outlet for the booming mining towns. It has been in continuous use since 1882. In the center of the rugged San Juan mining district, Silverton was once a booming mountain town. Buildings such as the Grand Imperial Hotel, a showplace of silver kings in the 1880's, and the gold-domed courthouse give evidence of the former prosperity of Silverton. Blair Street, with its false-front buildings, is used as a setting for many movies. It is the combination of this great historical role and scenic vistas unexcelled on any railway line in the United States that has turned the forty-five-mile line into Colorado's most important attraction and has assured its preservation as the most successful common-carrier passenger service in American railroading. After the D.&R.G.W. was frustrated in its attempts to abandon the Silverton, it reversed its policy and spent over one million dollars, through its subsidiary Rio Grande Land, developing downtown Durango into a facsimile of frontier times which has met with a success not usually found in such attempts at "restoration." The entire economy of the region is so tied to the destinies of the three-foot gauge that Durango officially calls itself "the narrow-gauge capital of the world"—a gross exaggeration coined by zealous Durangoans whose railroad world ends at the Utah state line. It certainly holds the title in the United States, however, and names such as Narrow Gauge Avenue and Locomotive Motel abound. In spite of a good try at historical accuracy, including construction of steel coaches that closely match the original wooden equipment, the D.&R.G.W. had to fall into the trap implicit in the code of travesty which governs tourist roads. The Pullman-green coaches are now Kodak-yellow, and the application of diamond stacks has "restored the engines to their original 1890 appearance," according to the railroad. The engines were built in 1923. In the summer of 1966 the Silverton train carried 76,000 passengers in approximately one hundred days of operation, running an extra section almost every day, at a fare of $6.50 for adults and $5.50 for children. Number 476, *above*, pulls a train north toward Hermosa, and a train, *below*, heads south from Silverton along the bank of the Animas River, which frequently washed away large sections of the line.

Two photos, Ron Ziel

25
25
18
19

Golden State Steam

In California a number of steam roads were still operating in the sixties, a new tourist railroad seeming to spring up every time a legitimate carrier dieselized or was abandoned. In June, 1962, McCloud River 2-6-2 No. 25, *left,* led Yreka Western 2-8-2 No. 19 with a fan trip near Pondosa. Yreka Western Mikados Nos. 18 and 19, *lower left,* were fired up for a Pacific Locomotive Association special on October 31, 1964. The following winter saw McCloud River No. 25, *below,* in steam again, this time at Hambone Junction.

Three photos, Karl R. Koenig

A Fine Museum

Many groups of historians have performed laudatory tasks in preserving railroadiana, but few can match the Mid-Continent Railway Museum at North Freedom, Wisconsin, for hard work, surmounting of formidable obstacles, and conscientiousness. By 1967 the museum had acquired twelve steam locomotives and twenty-two other pieces of equipment. Already four engines were in operating shape and three more were slated for heavy repairs. Also at North Freedom was C.B.&Q's famous Mikado, No. 4960, being held for the Circus World Museum. The usual motive power is Mogul No. 9, *below,* which came from the Dardanelle & Russellville in Arkansas. The most important piece of equipment in the museum, and one of the finest engines preserved anywhere, is a ten-wheeler, *right,* No. 1 of the Warren & Ouachita Valley Railway. The 4-6-0 was built by Baldwin in 1906 and came to the Rock Island when that road absorbed the latter in 1949. Two members of the museum organization purchased the engine in 1965 from the Rock Island, which obviously had no idea of its value. She was fired up especially for the photographer to get this picture—an indication of the hospitality of the men at Mid-Continent.

Two photos, Ron Ziel

1
1

Tourist Roads

When the promoters of tourist attractions got hold of steam locomotives, the result was often horrendous. The machine which was largely responsible for the realization of the American Dream was debauched and humiliated, only to line the pockets of promoters who did not care for historical fact. Indian raids on trains are staged in North Carolina, locomotives built in 1943 are outfitted with phony balloon stacks and square headlights, and two 4-4-0's are so tastelessly rebuilt as to lose all identity save wheel arrangement.

The distinction between railroads covered in this chapter and elsewhere is, at best, hazy. The cars following Steamtown's and Roaring Camp & Big Tree's locomotives are the same gaudy yellow. The Arcade & Attica, in a moment of temporary folly, once cautioned passengers against "desperate cattle rustlers" lying in wait "to stage a mock holdup." The award for the most atrocious tourist enterprise of all goes to the Swamp Rabbit Railroad in South Carolina, reported to have in service excursion cars with such historical railroad names as *Flopsey, Mopsey,* and *Peter Cottontail.* Beginning, then, with the Roaring Camp operation, decent in the treatment of its narrow-gauge shay and Heisler, and impressive in its California redwoods, this chapter runs the gamut from the sublime to the ridiculous.

Three photos, Karl R. Koenig

DIXIANA
CAMP

Wilbur T. Golson

Robert F. Collins

Pacific Coast Tourist Lines

When the late Walt Disney, a lifelong railfan, created Disneyland, a steam railroad was included. Perhaps the handsomest of Disneyland's locomotives is No. 3, *left.* Keeping Oregon in the category of states with active steam (at least during the summer) is the Veronia, South Park & Sunset, whose initials are quite similar to the Spokane, Portland & Seattle, over whose tracks and trestles, *below,* it operates. When the California Western Railroad acquired a steam locomotive to augment its gasoline-mechanical "skunk" railcars, it turned to a semilegitimate diamond-shaped spark arrester. Callously painted red, engine No. 45, *right,* traverses the road between Willits and Fort Bragg as motive power for the Super Skunk, whose schedule, being common carrier, is found in the *Official Guide.*

Ed Freitas

Michael A. Eagleson

Two photos, Ron Ziel

Tourist Roads in the Keystone State

With ten steam railroads hauling tourists and excursions, the Commonwealth of Pennsylvania leads all other states in the renaissance of steam locomotives, a fact well acknowledged by state business and government publications. They range from such big steam operations as Rail Tours through short-line common carriers like Strasburg and New Hope & Ivyland to fan-and-business-operated weekend lines. The Everett Railroad features an ex-Moorehead & North Fork 2-6-2, *left,* which pulls gaudy yellow, red, and silver coaches. The Penn View Mountain Railroad, near Blairsville, *lower left,* runs a bright blue 0-6-0, and a consist typical of these vest-pocket lines. The mining town of Ashland has reopened an old mine with local capital, using a Vulcan narrow-gauge 0-4-0T, *below,* to re-create a little operation supposedly reminiscent of the Lokies which worked the coal fields at the turn of the century.

69

Two photos, Ron Ziel

Tasteless, Tedious, and Tortured

The proprietors of some steam operations feel that steam locomotives, as built, were somehow incomplete and that their austere countenances therefore require "restoration." The unfortunate results shown here are typical, alas, of some thirty or forty such steam operations around the United States. A big, squat, outside-frame 2-8-0, which once did battle with Alaskan snowdrifts on the narrow-gauge White Pass & Yukon, *left,* now sports artificial decorations as it runs the rails of the Black Hills Central in North Dakota. The Highlander Railroad in Maggie Valley, North Carolina, has converted several fine old wood cabooses into the most awkward and ridiculous excursion cars imaginable, *above.* Of course, the Heisler on the head end has received the usual insipid "beauty treatment." After importing an engaging little Henschel 0-4-0T from Europe, the owners of Steam Village at Gilford, New Hampshire, *below,* attempted to Americanize the engine by adding a cowcatcher to the buffer plates. The awkward result looks worse than it does on United States-built switch engines.

Daniel A. Foley

George H. Foster

The Purgatory of Steam

Had Dante encountered steam locomotives in his *Inferno*, they would probably have arrived via Georgia's Stone Mountain Scenic Railroad, a few miles east of Atlanta in a state park. The promoters of Stone Mountain purchased the historically rare pair of 4-4-0's from the condemned Paulson Spence collection in 1962, rebuilding them to run on the road which bills itself as the "Route of the Great Locomotive Chase," an allusion to the daring seizure, in 1862, of the locomotive *General* by a band of Union raiders. A comparison of Stone Mountain's "General II," *lower right,* with the actual *General* on page 33 will further illustrate the futility of taking a perfectly proportioned little engine such as No. 1, *below,* circa 1920, and attempting to give it the appearance of an engine over sixty years older. Just as hideous was the transformation of her sister, No. 2, *upper right,* from Spence's Louisiana Eastern into Stone Mountain's "Texas II," *above,* shown at the terminal. Even the references to the Great Locomotive Chase are misleading, for the usual shoot-'em-up's and Indians are the order of the day on this exercise in debauchery.

Wilbur T. Golson

Wilbur T. Golson

Ron Ziel

The Great Railroad War—1967 Style

When the transcontinental railways were being pushed westward a century ago, there were several "railroad wars" as rival lines fought for the best routes. The tourist railroad business was shaken to the very foundations of its hot dog stands when, in January, 1967, the Tweetsie Railroad of Blowing Rock, North Carolina, brought the Tootsie Railroad into court to change its name. The result of the court hearing was that Tweetsie's name, and its image as the infantile successor, *right,* to the beautiful narrow-gauge lines of the East Tennessee & Western North Carolina Railway, remained intact. More cautious was the Petticoat Junction Railroad at Panama City Beach, Florida, *above,* which sought permission from the producers of the popular television show before using its name. The cabbage stack on the ex-Argent Lumber Company Mogul is genuine, as are the neon and plastic signs on the buildings, which lend a real frontier flavor to this absurd operation.

Two photos, Ron Ziel

Three photos, Wilbur T. Golson

More Dixie High Jinks

The Goldrush, Pidgeon Forge, Gatlinburg & Western (ex-Rebel Railroad), *top*, owns an ex-White Pass 2-8-2 (built by the same family that owns Tweetsie). The veteran of the World War II campaign to keep the Japanese out of Alaska would look fairly decent save for that ludicrous stack. Six Flags over Texas Amusement Park, *above*, operates the *General Sam Houston*, an ex-Louisiana sugar plantation engine. A new narrow-gauge 4-4-0 from Crown Metal Products, *left*, waits for its first load of tourists at Cherokee, North Carolina. An interesting feature of this operation is a phony tunnel which was built as an extension of an existing rock cut. Alas, steam in the sixties!

A Canadian in Connecticut
Rushing through Connecticut countryside on rails of the New Haven Railroad, Canadian National's famous 4-8-4, No. 6218, pulls a fantrip far from home rails, April 16, 1967.

Gene Collora

6218

2102
Reading
Lines

Vincent Alvino

Two photos, Michael A. Eagleson

The End, at Last

When the Reading dropped the fire on its famous T-1 4-8-4 No. 2102, *left,* main-line steam was vanquished in the East. By April, 1967, the Mississippian, the last steam road of any consequence not related to the tourist business in the South, had gone under. 2-8-0 No. 77 is shown switching dead sister No. 76 and her diesel replacement, *above.* Shiny new diesel fuel storage tanks stood where coal had once been loaded in the tenders of the Consolidations. The last of Norfolk & Western's famous Y-6b's, No. 2189, *below,* awaited the scrapper's torch in Roanoke, Virginia. Built in 1952, she only saw eight years of active service, and waited almost that much longer to be scrapped. These three photographs illustrate the story of steam in the sixties. As the decade drew to a close, there were hardly a dozen steam locomotives in service that were not dependent, at least in part, on tourists and railfans. Compared with the thousand or so steam engines that were still in useful service on North American railroads in 1960, the final curtain had indeed descended on the American continent. There was almost nothing left.

Howard Serig

The Elusive Ghost

As late as 1966, an ex-Illinois Central 0-8-0 switched the Traxler Gravel Co. yard at Crystal Springs, Mississippi. Her existence was almost completely unknown outside of the county in which she worked—a rare circumstance in the mid-1960's, when even the smallest of tank engines was kept under constant vigil by the railfans, who went everywhere in search of steam. The 3571 and several other ex-IC steam locomotives worked and were retired here, almost unremarked by the enthusiasts, who would have descended en masse upon the Traxler yard had they known of the treasure it concealed so well from the outside world.